AQA GCSE (9-1) Chemistry

Grade 5 Booster Workbook

For Combined Science: Trilogy

Dorothy Warren
Gemma Young

William Collins' dream of knowledge for all began with the publication of his first book in 1819. A self-educated mill worker, he not only enriched millions of lives, but also founded a flourishing publishing house. Today, staying true to this spirit, Collins books are packed with inspiration, innovation and practical expertise. They place you at the centre of a world of possibility and give you exactly what you need to explore it.

Collins. Freedom to teach

HarperCollins Publishers
The News Building
1 London Bridge Street
London SE1 9GF

HarperCollins*Publishers*
Macken House, 39/40 Mayor Street Upper
Dublin 1, D01 C9W8, Ireland

**Browse the complete Collins catalogue at
www.collins.co.uk**

10 9 8 7 6 5

© HarperCollins Publishers 2018

ISBN 978-0-00-829654-4

Collins® is a registered trademark of HarperCollins Publishers Limited

www.collins.co.uk

A catalogue record for this book is available from the British Library

Commissioned by Joanna Ramsay and Rachael Harrison
Development edited by Gillian Lindsey
Project managed by Sarah Thomas, Siobhan Brown and Mike Appleton
Copy edited by Jan Schubert and Aidan Gill
Proofread by Karen Roberts
Answer check by Angela Gardner
Typeset by Jouve India Pvt Ltd.,
Cover design by We are Laura and Jouve
Cover image: Arsenis Spyros/Shutterstock, Shutterstock/Zolnierek
Production by Tina Paul
Printed and Bound in the UK by Ashford Colour Press Ltd

Photo acknowledgement. p73/76 Martyn F. Chillmaid/Science Photo Library

MIX
Paper | Supporting responsible forestry
FSC™ C007454

This book contains FSC™ certified paper and other controlled sources to ensure responsible forest management.

For more information visit: www.harpercollins.co.uk/green

Contents

Introduction

This workbook will help you build your confidence in answering Chemistry questions for GCSE Combined Science.

It gives you practice in using key scientific words, writing longer answers, answering synoptic questions as well as applying knowledge and analysing information.

> Higher Tier content is clearly marked throughout.

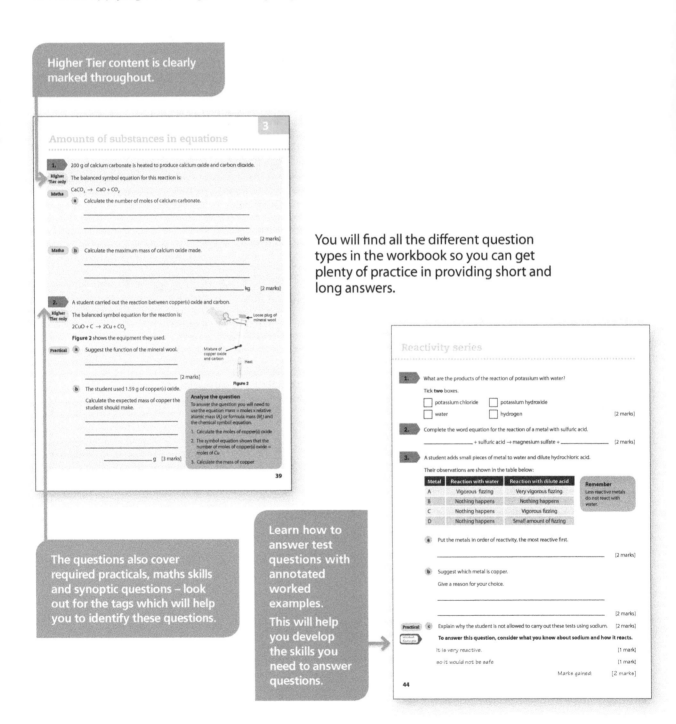

You will find all the different question types in the workbook so you can get plenty of practice in providing short and long answers.

> The questions also cover required practicals, maths skills and synoptic questions – look out for the tags which will help you to identify these questions.

> Learn how to answer test questions with annotated worked examples.
>
> This will help you develop the skills you need to answer questions.

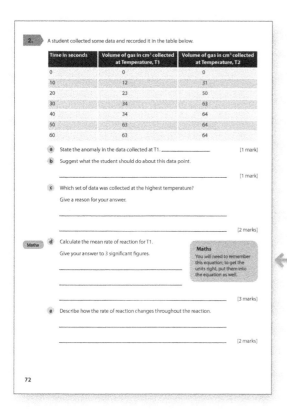

The amount of support gradually decreases throughout the workbook. As you build your skills you should be able to complete more of the questions yourself.

There are answers to all the questions at the back of the book. You can check your answers yourself or your teacher might tear them out and give them to you later to mark your work.

Atoms, elements and compounds

1. Which of these is an element?

Tick **one** box.

☐ Oxygen ☐ Water

☐ Air ☐ Carbon dioxide

[1 mark]

> **Remember**
> Elements are listed on the periodic table. You will be supplied with one in the exam.

2. Write the symbol or formula for each element.

Worked Example

Atom of sodium Na   Marks gained: [0.5 marks]

Atom of calcium _____

Molecule of oxygen O_2 Marks gained: [0.5 marks]

Molecule of chlorine _____   [1 mark]

3. Iron can be extracted from iron oxide by reacting it with carbon. The products are iron and carbon dioxide.

a Name two elements mentioned.

1 _____   2 _____   [2 marks]

b Name two compounds mentioned.

1 _____   2 _____   [2 marks]

4. Define what a compound is

_____

_____

_____   [2 marks]

> **Command word**
> Define means to state the meaning of something. So, in this question you need to say what a compound is.

Mixtures

1.

Synoptic

Draw **one** line from each diagram to the description. [4 marks]

Diagram | Description

A pure compound

A pure element

A mixture of elements

A mixture of compounds

2.

Practical

A student is given a mixture of iron filings and sulfur powder.

a Suggest a suitable way of separating the iron and sulfur.

Describe how the technique will work.

_____

_____ [2 marks]

b The student heats the mixture to form iron sulfide.

Explain why it is easy to separate the iron and sulfur in the mixture, but not in the compound.

_____

_____

_____ [2 marks]

Compounds, formulae and equations

1. Sodium nitrate contains three oxygen atoms and one nitrogen atom for every sodium atom.

What is its formula?

Tick **one** box.

☐ NaN_3O ☐ $NNaO_3$ ☐ O_3NaN ☐ $NaNO_3$ [1 mark]

2. Draw one line from each formula to the compound it represents.

Worked Example

Formula		Compound
Fe_2O_3		Magnesium sulfide
KI		Magnesium sulfate
MgS		Potassium iodide
$MgSO_4$		Iron oxide

[4 marks]

3. The gas freon-11 has the formula CCl_2F.

Name the elements it contains.

1 _____   2 _____   3 _____   [3 marks]

4. Metals react with acids to produce a salt and hydrogen.

Complete the word and symbol equations to show an example.

magnesium + hydrochloric acid → _____ + hydrogen

_____ + 2HCl → $MgCl_2$ + _____   [4 marks]

> **Remember**
> Some tips for writing symbol equations:
> Use the periodic table supplied to find the symbols of elements
> Elements that are gases at room temperature (other than the group 0 elements) exist as pairs e.g. O_2
> Symbol equations must be balanced. You can only change the number in front of the formulae
> You may be asked to provide state symbols (s, l, g, aq)

Scientific models of the atom

1. **Figure 1** is a diagram of an early model of the atom.

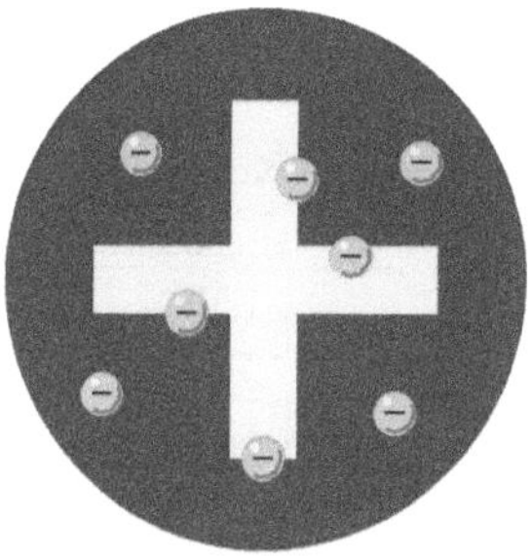

a Name the model.

Tick **one** box.

☐ nuclear model ☐ billiard ball model

☐ plum pudding model ☐ Bohr model [1 mark]

Figure 1

b Use the words in the box to complete the sentence about this model.

| electrons | negatively | neutrally | neutrons | positively | protons |

The atom is a _____ charged ball with _____

charged particles called _____ in it. [3 marks]

2. In 1909, scientists carried out the alpha particle scattering experiment to test this model **(Figure 1)**.

- They made a prediction based on the model.

- They carried out the experiment.

- The results did not agree with their prediction.

- The experiment was repeated by other scientists. They got the same results.

Literacy

When you are asked to explain something, write down the reasons why it happens.

You will get marks for how clear your answer is as well as using key terms correctly. Some that you might use are: evidence, data, validity, reproducible.

Explain why this experiment led to a change in the model of the atom.

_____

_____

_____

_____

_____

_____

_____ [6 marks]

Sizes of atoms and molecules

1.

Maths

Draw **one** line from each number to the same number in standard form.

Number	Standard form
1000	1×10^6
100	1.1×10^4
11 000	1×10^3
1 million	1×10^2

Maths

Because atoms are very small, standard form is used to show their size.

You need to be able to use numbers when in the standard form.

[4 marks]

2.

Maths

Nanometres (nm) are a unit of measurement.

$1 \text{ nm} = 1 \times 10^{-9} \text{ m}$

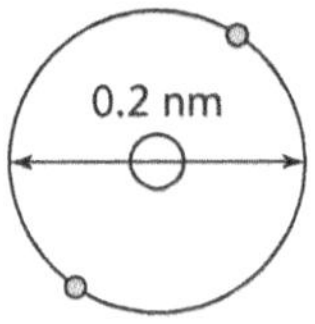

Figure 2 shows the diameter of a hydrogen atom.

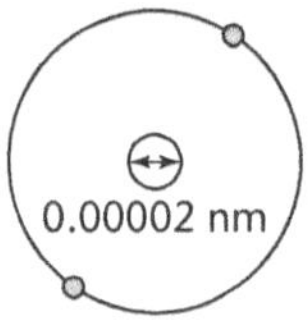

What is 0.2 nm in metres?

0.2 nm

0.00002 nm

Figure 2   **Figure 3**

Tick **one** box.

☐ 1×10^{-2} m   ☐ 1×10^{-10} m   ☐ 2×10^{-9} m   ☐ 2×10^{-10} m   [1 mark]

3.

Worked Example

Figure 3 shows the diameter of the nucleus.

Use the information in Figures 2 and 3 to calculate how many times larger the diameter of the atom is than the diameter of the nucleus.   [2 marks]

$$\frac{0.2 \text{ (diameter of the whole atom)}}{0.00002 \text{ (diameter of the nucleus)}} = 10\ 000$$

The diameter of the atom is 10 000 times larger than the diameter of the nucleus   Marks gained: [2 marks]

4.

Maths

A teacher uses a circular sports stadium as a **scale model** of the hydrogen atom.

The stadium has a diameter of 150 m.

The nucleus is modelled by a sphere in the centre of the stadium.

Using information from Q3, calculate the diameter that the sphere needs to be **in mm**.

_____ mm   [3 marks]

Relative masses and charges of subatomic particles

1. **Figure 4** is a model of an atom.

   a Complete the table to show the names and relative charge on the particles in an atom.

Letter on diagram	Name of particle	Relative charge
X		0
Y		+1
Z		

   [4 marks]

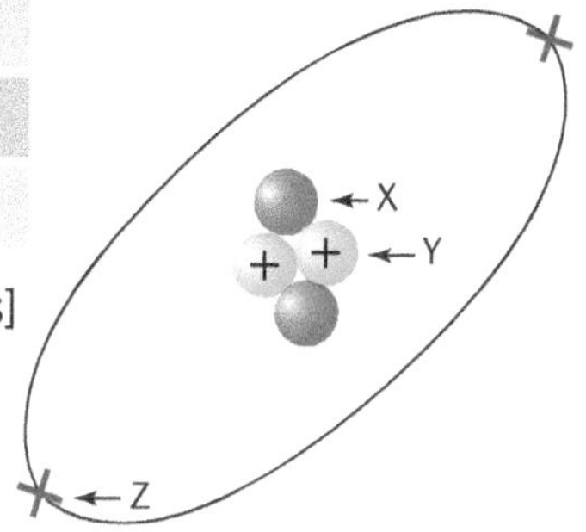

   b Atoms have no overall charge.

   Which sentence explains why?

   Tick **one** box.

   ☐ There are the same number of negative and positive particles in the nucleus.

   ☐ The charge on the neutrons cancels out the charges on the other particles.

   ☐ They contain the same number of protons and electrons.

   ☐ They contain the same number of neutrons and electrons. [1 mark]

   c For the atom in **Figure 4**, state its:

   i Atomic number _____   **ii** Mass number _____

   iii Symbol _____ [3 marks]

   Figure 4

2. **Figure 5** shows two different isotopes of carbon.

   Compare the numbers of particles in the atoms of each isotope.

   $^{12}_{6}C$ $^{14}_{6}C$

   Carbon-12   Carbon-14

   Figure 5

   _____

   _____

   _____

   _____

   [4 marks]

   Command word

   When you are asked to **compare** you need to describe similarities and differences.

   You must write about both things, not just one.

Relative atomic mass

1. The nucleus of an atom contains 11 protons and 12 neutrons.

Synoptic Which statements about the atom are true?

Tick **two** boxes.

☐ It has a mass number of 23.   ☐ It has a mass number of 12.

☐ It has an atomic number of 11.   ☐ It has an atomic number of 12.   [2 marks]

2. Bromine has two isotopes: $^{79}_{35}$Br (bromine -79) and $^{81}_{35}$Br (bromine-81).

a How many neutrons does bromine-81 contain?

Tick **one** box.

☐ 35   ☐ 46   ☐ 81   ☐ 116   [1 mark]

Worked Example

Maths

b In any sample of bromine, 50% would be bromine-79 atoms and 50% would be bromine-81 atoms.

Calculate the relative atomic mass of bromine.   [3 marks]

> **Common misconception**
>
> Not all atoms of one element have the same mass number. The relative atomic mass is an average value that takes account of the abundance of the isotopes of the element.

First, multiple the mass number of each isotope by the relative abundance (the percentage)

Bromine–79 = 79 × 50 = 3950

Bromine–81 = 81 × 50 = 4050   [1 mark]

Then, add these numbers together and divide by 100:

(3950 + 4050) / 100   [1 mark]

The relative atomic mass of bromine is 80:   [1 mark]

           Marks gained: [3 marks]

3. Chlorine has two isotopes: ^{35}Cl and ^{37}Cl.

Maths In any sample of chlorine, 75 % of the atoms are ^{35}Cl and 25 % are ^{37}Cl.

Calculate the relative atomic mass of chlorine.   [3 marks]

Relative atomic mass of chlorine = _____   [1 mark]

4. Define what relative atomic mass means.

_____

_____ [2 marks]

Electronic structure

1. Draw **one** line from each element to its electronic structure.

Element   Electronic structure

| Boron |
| Atomic number = 5 |

| Hydrogen |
| Atomic number = 1 |

| Neon |
| Atomic number = 10 |

| Carbon |
| Atomic number = 6 |

Analysing the question
To work out electronic structure you need to know the atomic number of the element. This will tell you how many electrons each atom has and where it can be found on the periodic table.

[4 marks]

2. Use the words in the box to complete the sentences.

| eight   energy   nucleus   one   shell   two |

Electrons in an atom orbit the _____ in _____ levels.

An atom can hold _____ electrons in the lowest level and _____ in the second level.

[4 marks]

3. A sodium atom has an atomic number of 11.

When a sodium atom loses its outermost electron it forms a sodium ion.

a In the space to the right draw a diagram to show the electronic structure of a sodium ion. [2 marks]

b Explain why a sodium ion has a positive charge.

_____

_____

_____

_____ [2 marks]

Electronic structure and the periodic table

1. How are the elements arranged in the periodic table?

Tick **one** box.

☐ In order of atomic number.　　☐ In order of mass number.

☐ In order of reactivity.　　☐ In order of number of neutrons. [1 mark]

2. Why do elements in the same group of the periodic table have similar chemical properties?

Tick **one** box.

☐ They have the same atomic number.　　☐ They have the same reactivity.

☐ They have the same number of electrons on their outer shell.　　☐ They are the same size. [1 mark]

3. **Figure 6** shows the periodic table. Some elements are shown by letters.

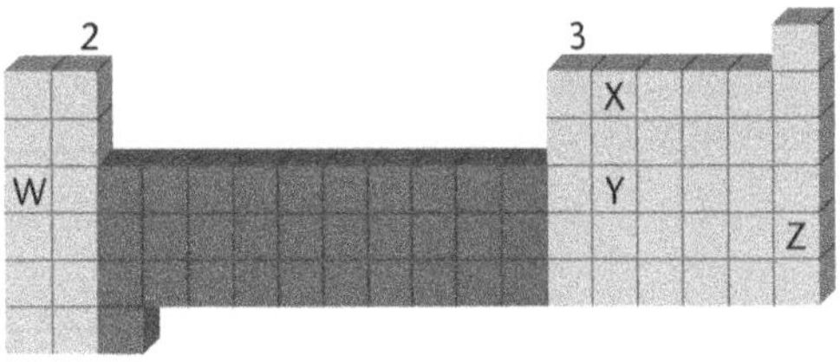

Figure 6

a The atoms of which element (W, X, Y or Z) has:

i One electron on its outer shell? _____

ii A full outer shell of electrons? _____

iii The highest atomic number? _____

iv The fewest protons? _____ [4 marks]

b Which two elements (W, X, Y or Z) have the same number of electrons on their outer shell?

_____ and _____ [1 mark]

Development of the periodic table

1. Use the words in the box to complete the sentences.

| reactivity   atomic weight   groups   atomic number   rows |

In 1869 Dmitri Mendeleev produced an early version of the periodic table.

He arranged the elements in order of their _____

He then placed elements with similar properties into _____ [2 marks]

2. When the next element did not follow the pattern Mendeleev left a gap.

Table 1 shows an example is in group 3.

Table 1

Row	Element	Metal or non-metal	Melting point in °C	Density in g/cm³	Formula of chloride compound
1	Boron	Metal	2076	2.34	BCl_3
2	Aluminium	Metal	660	2.70	$AlCl_3$
3	X				

Predict the properties of the missing element, X, in group 3.

_____

_____

_____

_____ [4 marks]

Analysing the question

You know that there are patterns in the elements as you go down a group, for example melting point may increase as you go down a group.

Look at the patterns in the two elements in the table and use the data to state what the properties of the missing element could be.

Comparing metals and non-metals

1. **Figure 7** is a diagram of the periodic table.

   Shade the area to show where **non-metals** are found. [1 mark]

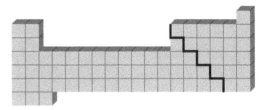

   Figure 7

2. Sodium reacts with chlorine to form sodium chloride.

   a Write a word equation to show this reaction.

   _____ [1 mark]

   b Draw **one** line from each substance to the correct description.

   Substance   Description

   | Sodium | | Metal |

   | Sodium chloride | | Non-metal |

   | Chlorine | [3 marks]

3. **Table 2** shows physical properties of different elements.

   Table 2

Element	Does it conduct electricity?	Melting point in °C	Boiling point in °C	Density in g/cm³
A	Yes	180.5	1342	0.53
B	No	−7.2	58.8	3.10
C	No	115.2	444.6	2.07
D	Yes	419.5	907	7.13

   a Which elements (A, B, C or D) are non-metals?

   _____ and _____ [2 marks]

   b Which element (A, B, C or D) is a liquid at room temperature? _____ [1 mark]

   c State **two** physical properties that the metals in **Table 2** share.

   1 _____   2 _____ [2 marks]

Elements in group 0

1. Which statements are true about **all** elements in group 0?

Tick **two** boxes.

☐ They exist as single atoms.

☐ They have 8 electrons on their outer shell.

☐ They have a full outer shell of electrons.

☐ They have high melting and boiling points.

[2 marks]

2. **Table 3** shows data on the group 0 elements.

Table 3

Element	Helium	Neon	Argon	Krypton	Xenon	Radon
Atomic number	2	10	18	36	54	86
Density (g/dm³)	0.18	0.90	1.78	3.71	5.85	9.97

Maths **a** Calculate the mass of 10 dm³ of argon. Give your answer to 2 significant figures.

_____ g   [2 marks]

Maths **b** Plot the data on the graph axes on **Figure 8**.

Draw a line of best fit.   [3 marks]

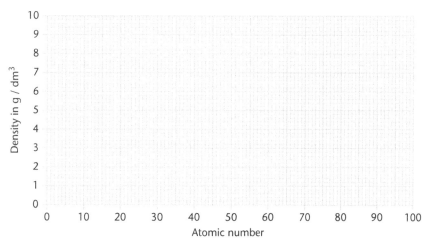

Figure 8

3. Use electronic structure to explain why elements in group 0 of the periodic table are unreactive.

_____

_____ [3 marks]

Elements in group 1

A teacher demonstrates the reactions of the group 1 metals with water.

1. The group 1 metals are also known as:

Tick **one** box.

☐ The halogens   ☐ The noble gases

☐ The alkali metals   ☐ The transition metals   [1 mark]

2. First, they cut a piece of lithium from a larger block.

Practical The students observe that the cut surface of lithium is shiny but it slowly goes dull.

a Name the element that the lithium is reacting with when it becomes dull. [1 mark]

b They put the piece of lithium into the water.

Complete the word equation for the reaction that takes place.

lithium + water → _____ + _____ [2 marks]

c State **one** safety precaution they will take when carrying out this demonstration.

_____ [1 mark]

3. The teacher then cuts a piece of sodium.

Sodium is found below lithium in group 1 of the periodic table.

Tick the correct statement.

☐ The sodium will go dull more quickly than lithium because it is more reactive.

☐ The sodium will go dull more slowly than lithium because it is less reactive. [1 mark]

4. Compare the reaction of sodium and lithium with water.

_____

_____

_____

_____ [4 marks]

Elements in group 7

1. Bromine is found in group 7 of the periodic table. Its formula is Br_2.

What does this tell you about bromine?

Tick **one** box.

☐ Bromide ions have a charge of −2.

☐ There are always 2 bromine atoms in a compound.

☐ Bromine exists as pairs of atoms.

☐ Bromine is a reactive element. [1 mark]

2. Use the information in **Table 4** to answer the following questions.

Table 4

	Name of element	Melting point in °C	Boiling point in °C
Increase in atomic number →	fluorine	−220	−188
	chlorine	−102	−34
	bromine	−7	59
	iodine		184

a Name **one** group 7 element that is a gas at room temperature.

_____ [1 mark]

b Describe the trend in boiling points as you go down the group.

_____ [1 mark]

3. **Figure 9** shows the electronic structure of the first three group 7 elements.

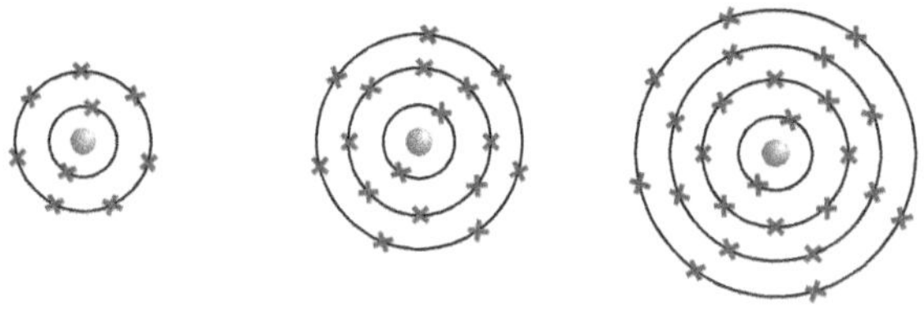

Figure 9

Literacy Use the diagrams to explain why the reactivity of the halogens decreases as you go down the group.

_____

_____

_____

_____

_____

_____

_____

_____

_____ [6 marks]

4. During a displacement reaction a more reactive halogen displaces a less reactive halogen from a solution of its salt.

a Complete the equation:

chlorine + potassium bromide → _____ + _____ [2 marks]

b When iodine is added to a solution of potassium bromide, no changes are observed. Explain why.

_____

_____ [2 marks]

18

The three states of matter

1. Copper oxide is a solid. It reacts with dilute sulfuric acid to form a solution of copper sulfate.

Which symbol equation correctly shows the state symbols for this reaction?

Remember

(aq) stands for 'aqueous', which means a solution of a soluble substance in water.

Tick **one** box. [1 mark]

☐ $CuO (s) + H_2SO_4 (l) \rightarrow CuSO_4 (aq) + H_2O (l)$

☐ $CuO (s) + H_2SO_4 (aq) \rightarrow CuSO_4 (s) + H_2O (l)$

☐ $CuO (s) + H_2SO_4 (aq) \rightarrow CuSO_4 (aq) + H_2O (l)$

☐ $CuO (s) + H_2SO_4 (l) \rightarrow CuSO_4 (aq) + H_2O (aq)$

2. In **Figure 1** each change of state is shown by a letter.

Write the correct letter (A, B, C or D) in the box next to each change of state.

Boiling ☐ Condensing ☐

Freezing ☐ Melting ☐ [4 marks]

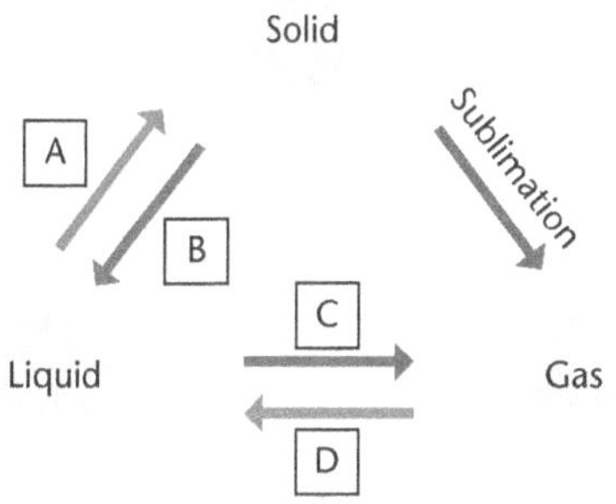

Solid

A

B

C

Sublimation

Liquid Gas

D

Figure 1

3. A student wanted to find out the melting point of the compound salol.

This is the method they used:

1. Put two spatulas of salol into a boiling tube and add a thermometer.

2. Put the boiling tube in a hot water bath.

Practical **a** Describe how they would measure the melting point of salol.

_____

_____

_____ [2 marks]

b They could not measure the melting point of magnesium oxide in school.

Suggest why.

_____

_____ [2 marks]

19

Ionic bonding and ionic compounds

1. Which of the following compounds are ionic?

Tick **two** boxes.

☐ sodium chloride (NaCl) ☐ carbon dioxide (CO_2)

☐ lithium oxide (Li_2O) ☐ hydrogen chloride (HCl) [2 marks]

2. Calcium oxide (CaO) is an ionic compound.

a What ions does it contain?

Tick **one** box.

☐ Ca^+ and O^- ☐ Ca^+ and O^{2-} ☐ Ca^{2+} and O^- ☐ Ca^{2+} and O^{2-} [1 mark]

b **Figure 2** shows two ball and stick diagrams (A and B).

A   B   **Figure 2**

i Which diagram represents calcium oxide? [1 mark]

_____

> **Remember**
> You can count the number of each types of ion to give you an estimate of the ratio.
>
> It won't be an exact number because this is just one part of a much bigger structure. The ions on the sides and corners are bonded to other ions that are not included in the image.

Worked Example

ii Explain your choice. [1 mark]

The formula of calcium oxide is CaO
(this is given above)

Marks gained: [1 mark]

In B there are 14 of the large spheres 13 of the smaller ones.

This is approximately a ratio of 1:1, so it must contain 1 calcium ion to every 1 oxide ion.

> **Analyse the question**
> Use the periodic table to find what groups potassium and sulfur are in.
>
> Use this to work out the charge on their ions.
>
> The charge on the compound needs to be neutral.

3. State the formula for the ionic compound potassium sulfide.

_____ [2 marks]

Dot and cross diagrams for ionic compounds

1. The substance magnesium fluoride is made up of Mg^{2+} and F^- ions.

a What type of bonding occurs in magnesium fluoride?

Tick **one** box.

☐ Covalent   ☐ Hydrogen   ☐ Ionic   ☐ Metallic   [1 mark]

b What is the formula of magnesium fluoride?

Tick **one** box.

☐ MgF   ☐ Mg^2F ☐ Mg_2F ☐ MgF_2 [1 mark]

2. **Figure 3** shows an atom of sodium and an atom of oxygen.

Na   O   **Figure 3**

Describe what happens when sodium reacts with oxygen to form the compound sodium oxide.

_____

_____

_____

_____

_____

_____ [5 marks]

> **Analyse the question**
> This question is worth 5 marks so try and include as much detail as you can. Describe what will happen to the electrons and what ions will be formed.

Properties of ionic compounds

1. Which statement is **true** about ionic compounds?

Tick **two** boxes.

☐ They have low boiling points.

☐ They have high boiling points.

☐ They are all gases at room temperature.

☐ They are all solids at room temperature.

Remember

The ions in ionic compounds are bonded very strongly to each other by ionic bonds.

A lot of energy is required to break them.

[2 marks]

2. **Figure 4** shows a 2D diagram of the structure of an ionic compound.

Only some of the charges on the ions are shown.

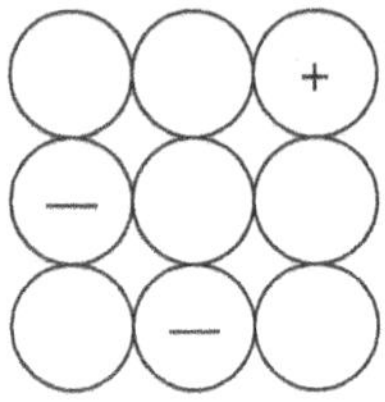

a Draw in the rest of the charges to complete the diagram. [1 mark]

b What do we call this type of structure?

Figure 4

Tick **one** box.

☐ Giant covalent structure   ☐ Giant ionic lattice

☐ A polymer   ☐ Giant molecular structure   [1 mark]

3. Sodium chloride is an ionic compound.

Literacy It has a high melting point.

It will not conduct electricity when solid but will when melted.

Use what you know about the structure of sodium chloride to explain these properties.

_____

_____

_____

_____

_____

_____ [6 marks]

Covalent bonding in small molecules

1. Which substances are made up of small molecules?

Tick **two** boxes.

☐ Gold ☐ Carbon dioxide ☐ Water ☐ Aluminium oxide [2 marks]

2. Use the words in the box to complete the sentence about covalent bonding.

electrons	full	protons	share	strong	transfer	weak

A covalent bond is formed when atoms _____ pairs of _____.

The covalent bonds between atoms are _____. [3 marks]

3. **Figure 5** is a diagram of one molecule of a covalent substance.

Worked Example

a State the chemical formula of the substance. [1 mark]

H_2O Marks gained: [1 mark]

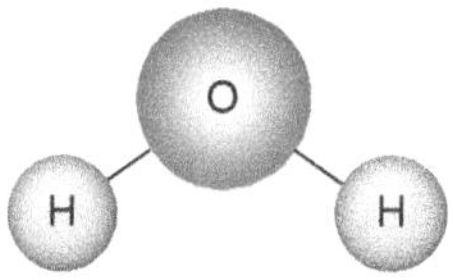

Figure 5

> **Remember**
> When you write a formula of a compound the symbol of the metal or hydrogen is placed first.
> Small subscript numbers $_{like\ this}$ are placed after the symbols to show how many of each atom are present.
> You might need to add brackets – for example there are two nitrate (NO_3) ions in $Mg(NO_3)_2$
> Without the brackets it would be $MgNO_{32}$, which means there are 32 oxygen atoms!

b Name the substance. _____ [1 mark]

4. Methane has the formula CH_4.

Complete the diagram below by drawing **lines** to show the bonds in methane. [1 mark]

```
      H
  H   C   H
      H
```

Dot and cross diagrams for covalent compounds

1. Some substances are made up of small covalent molecules.

Draw **one** line from each covalent molecule to the diagram which shows its structure.

Covalent molecule   **Structure**

Ammonia (NH$_3$)

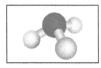

Methane (CH$_4$)

Chlorine (Cl$_2$)

Hydrogen chloride (HCl)

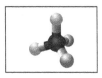

[4 marks]

2. **Figure 6** shows how the outer electrons are arranged in an atom of hydrogen and an atom of chlorine.

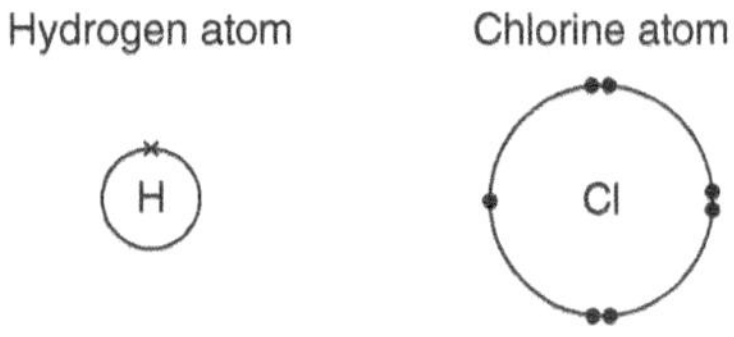

Hydrogen atom   Chlorine atom

Figure 6

a Draw a diagram to show how the atoms are arranged in a molecule of hydrogen chloride. [3 marks]

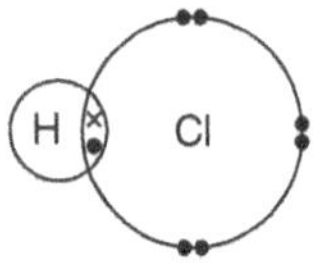

Marks gained: [3 marks]

b A dot and cross diagram is not a true representation of the structure of a small molecule.

Give **one** reason why.

_____ [1 mark]

3. **Figure 7** shows how the outer electrons are arranged in an atom of nitrogen.

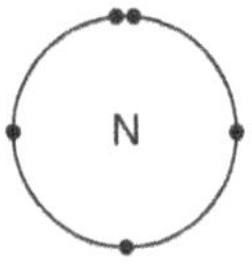

Figure 7

Complete **Figure 8** to show how the electrons are arranged in a molecule of nitrogen (N$_2$). [2 marks]

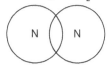

Figure 8

> **Remember**
> In some molecules, more than one pair of electrons are shared.

24

Properties of small molecules

1. Which are properties of small molecules?

Tick **two** boxes.

☐ Normally gases or liquids at room temperature

☐ Normally solids at room temperature

☐ Relatively high melting and boiling points

☐ Do not conduct electricity when dissolved in water

Common misconception

It is important to remember that the intermolecular bonds between small molecules are weak.

But, the covalent bonds between the atoms in the molecules are very strong.

2. The alkanes are a family of molecules.

Methane (CH_4) and ethane (C_2H_6) are both alkanes.

Alkanes contain atoms of which two elements?

1 _____   2 _____   [2 marks]

3. What type of bonding exists between the atoms in alkane molecules?

Tick **one** box.

☐ Covalent   ☐ Ionic   ☐ Intermolecular   ☐ Metallic   [1 mark]

4. A liquid alkane is heated until it becomes a gas.

Which sentence explains what happens?

Tick **one** box.

☐ The bonds between the atoms in the molecules break.

☐ The forces between the molecules (intermolecular forces) break.

☐ The molecules become atoms.

☐ The molecules become ions.   [1 mark]

Polymers

1. Which material is made from polymers?

Tick **one** box.

☐ Sodium chloride ☐ Diamond ☐ Plastic ☐ Steel   [1 mark]

2. **Figure 9** shows two polymer chains.

Draw **one** intermolecular force.   [1 mark]

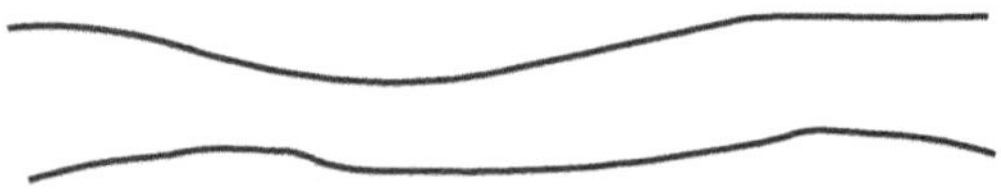

Figure 9

> **Remember**
> **Inter**molecular means between molecules.
> **Intra**molecular means between the atoms in molecules.

3. Poly(ethene) is a polymer made from the gas ethene.

Poly(ethene) is a solid at room temperature. Ethene is a gas.

Explain why.

Use the strength of their intermolecular forces in your answer.

_____

_____

_____   [3 marks]

4. A student studied the physical properties of two polymers.

Polymer A was hard and rigid. It could not be stretched.

Polymer B could be stretched a little before breaking.

a Identify the polymer, A or B, which contains covalent cross-links between

the polymer chains. _____   [1 mark]

b Explain the reason for your answer.

_____

_____

_____   [2 marks]

Giant covalent structures

1. Simple molecules and giant covalent structures are both covalently bonded.

Some examples are shown below.

| ammonia | diamond | graphite | oxygen | silicon dioxide | water |

a Complete **Table 1** but writing the names of the examples into the correct columns. [4 marks]

Table 1

Simple molecules	Giant covalent structure
Water	Diamond

Synoptic **b** State **one** example from **Table 1** that is:

i An element _____ [1 mark]

ii A gas at room temperature _____ [1 mark]

iii Made up of carbon atoms only _____ [1 mark]

2. **Figure 10** shows three examples of giant covalent structures.

Name each one. [3 marks]

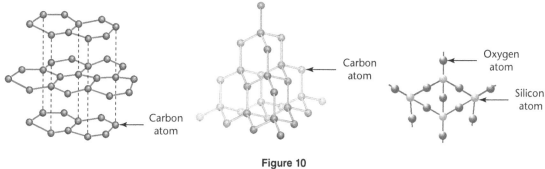

Figure 10

_____   _____   _____

3. Silicon dioxide (SiO_2) and carbon dioxide (CO_2) are both covalent compounds.

Compare their structures.

You should describe the bonding between the atoms in each.

_____

_____

_____

_____   [4 marks]

Properties of giant covalent structures

1. Which is a property that **all** giant covalent structures have?

Tick **one** box.

> **Remember**
> All the bonds in a giant covalent structure are very strong.

☐ Able to conduct electricity

☐ High melting and boiling point

☐ Hard

☐ Strong [1 mark]

2. Diamond is the hardest naturally occurring substance on Earth.

Figure 11 shows its structure.

Explain why diamond is hard.

You should use what you know about its structure and bonding.

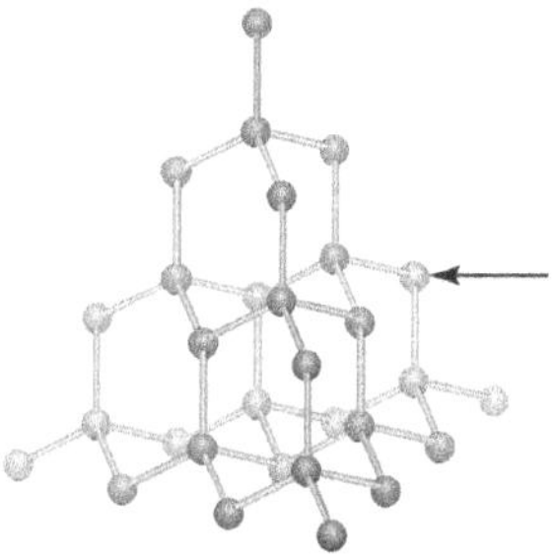

← Carbon atom

Figure 11

_____

_____ [2 marks]

3. **Figure 12** shows the structure of graphite.

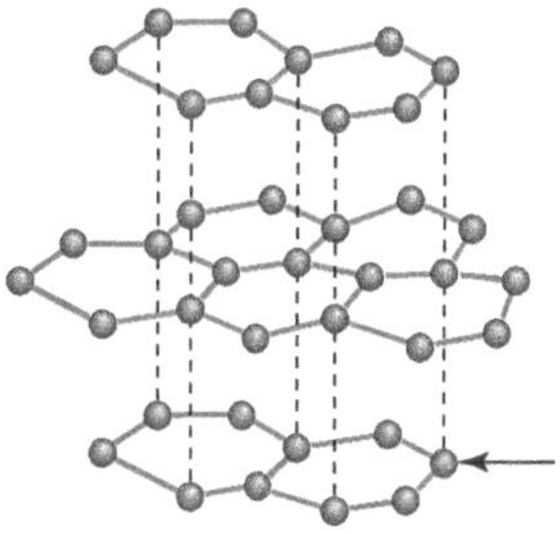

a State **one** similarity between the structure of diamond and graphite.

_____ [1 mark]

← Carbon atom

Figure 12

b Graphite is a soft material that can conduct electricity. [2 marks]

What other substance can conduct electricity?

☐ Polymer   ☐ Metal   ☐ Silicon dioxide   ☐ Diamond   [1 mark]

c Explain why graphite can conduct electricity.

_____

_____ [2 marks]

Graphene and fullerenes

1. This question is about carbon structures.

a Select **two** words from the box to name the structures below.

Carbon nanotube   Diamond   Graphite   Graphene

Structure A _____   Structure B _____   [2 marks]

b How many carbon atoms are in each ring in structure A? _____ [1 mark]

c State **one** use of structure B.

_____ [1 mark]

d Explain why its properties make it suitable for this use.

_____

_____ [2 marks]

2. Carbon nanotubes are a type of fullerene.

Maths **a** The width of one type of carbon nanotube is 10 nm.

What is this in metres?

Tick **one** box.

☐ 1×10^{-6} m   ☐ 1×10^{-7} m   ☐ 1×10^{-8} m   ☐ 1×10^{-9} m   [1 mark]

b It has a width:length ratio of 1:100 000

How long is the carbon nanotube **in mm**?

1 nm $= 0.000001$ mm

_____ mm   [3 marks]

> **Remember**
> You need to be able to use prefixes so try and remember what they mean.
> 1 nm $= 1 \times 10^{-9}$ m.

Metallic bonding

1. The atoms in which substances are held together by metallic bonding?

Tick **two** boxes.

☐ Carbon   ☐ Carbon dioxide   ☐ Cobalt   ☐ Copper   [2 marks]

2. What is true about metallic bonding?

Tick **one** box.

☐ It is weak   ☐ It is strong   ☐ It is covalent   ☐ It is ionic   [1 mark]

3. **Figure 13** shows metallic bonding.

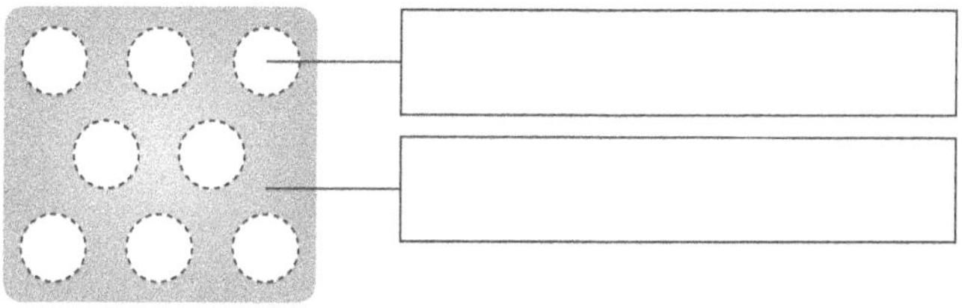

Figure 13

Choose the correct labels from the list below to label it.

negative ion   positive ion   sea of electrons   sea of protons

[2 marks]

4. The electrons in a metal are delocalised.

What does this mean?

_____

_____

_____   [2 marks]

5. Explain why the atoms in a metal are held tightly together.

_____

_____

_____

_____   [3 marks]

Properties of metals and alloys

1. Which substance is an alloy?

Tick **one** box.

☐ aluminium   ☐ bronze   ☐ copper   ☐ zinc   [1 mark]

2. Define alloy.

_____   [2 marks]

3. **Figure 14** shows the structure of an alloy.

Explain why alloys are stronger than pure metals.

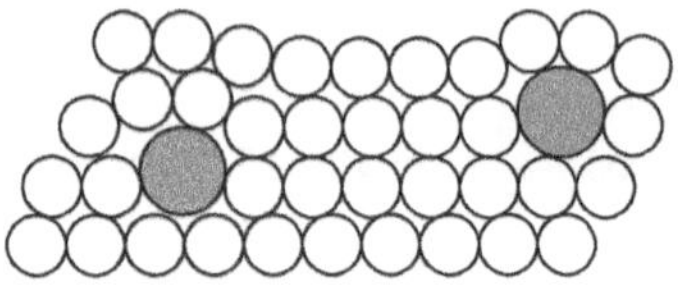

Figure 14

_____

_____   [2 marks]

4. The data in **Table 2** shows the melting points of metals found in group 1 and 2 of the periodic table.

Synoptic

Table 2

Metal	Melting point in °C
Calcium	842
Magnesium	650
Potassium	63
Sodium	98

a Use the data in **Table 2** to compare the melting point of group 1 and 2 metals.

_____

_____

[1 mark]

b In general, the more delocalised electrons there are in the metal, the stronger the metallic bonds.

Use the information to suggest an explanation for your answer to part **a**.

Use the electronic structure of the metals in your answer.

_____

_____

_____

_____   [4 marks]

Writing formulae

1. A molecule of boron fluoride contains 3 fluorine (F) atoms and 1 boron (B) atom.

What is the formula of boron fluoride?

Tick **one** box.

☐ B_3F ☐ BF_3 ☐ F3B   ☐ F_3B [1 mark]

2. Lead(IV) oxide is made up of Pb^{4+} and O^{2-} ions.

Write the formula for lead(IV) oxide.

_____   [1 mark]

3. Determine the number of hydrogen atoms in each of the following.

a NH_3 _____

b $2H_2O$ _____

c   [3 marks]

$$CH_3—\overset{\overset{\displaystyle CH_3}{|}}{\underset{\underset{\displaystyle Cl}{|}}{C}}—CH_2CH_3$$

4. A student reacts calcium carbonate with hydrochloric acid.

Practical The products of the reaction are calcium chloride, water and carbon dioxide.

Synoptic **a** Suggest how they could collect and measure the volume of carbon dioxide made.

_____

_____   [1 mark]

b Draw **one** line from the name of each substance to its formula.   [3 marks]

Substance   Formula

| Calcium carbonate | | CO_2 |

| Calcium chloride | | $CaCl_2$ |

| Carbon dioxide | | $CaCO_3$ |

Conservation of mass and balanced chemical equations

1. Draw a ring around the correct answer to complete each sentence.

The law of conservation of mass states that no atoms are

gained
rearranged
lost

or made

during a

physical change.
chemical reaction.
reversible change.

This means that the mass of the products is

less than
equal to
more than

the mass of the reactants.

[3 marks]

2. A student carries out a reaction: $A + B \rightarrow C$.

Maths They use 2.3 g of A and 1.2 g of B.

Calculate the expected mass of C.

_____

_____ [2 marks]

3. A student is asked to balance the symbol equation for the reaction of hydrogen and oxygen to make water.

$H_2 + O_2 \rightarrow H_2O$

This is their answer.

$H_2 + O_2 \rightarrow H_2O_2$

Explain why this is incorrect.

Write the correct answer.

> **Remember**
>
> When you balance an equation you cannot change the small (subscript) numbers. This changes the substance. For example, O_2 is oxygen, O_3 is the toxic gas ozone.
>
> However, you can change the number of atoms of each substance by adding a number in front of the formula. E.g. $2O_2$ contains 4 oxygen atoms.

_____

_____ [2 marks]

Mass changes when a reactant or product is a gas

1. When magnesium is burnt a white powder called magnesium oxide is formed.

The balanced symbol equation for the reaction is:

$2Mg + O_2 \rightarrow 2MgO$

Maths A student burns 3 g of magnesium. The mass of the magnesium oxide produced is 4.2 g.

Calculate the increase in mass.

_____

_____

_____ g   [1 mark]

2. A class carries out an experiment.

Practical They heat copper carbonate to form copper oxide and carbon dioxide.

Figure 1 shows the equipment they used.

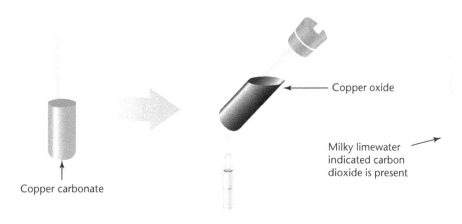

Copper oxide

Milky limewater indicated carbon dioxide is present

Copper carbonate

Figure 1

a What kind of reaction is this?

Tick **one** box.

☐ Combustion   ☐ Oxidation

☐ Neutralisation   ☐ Thermal decomposition   [1 mark]

b They use 4.6 g of copper carbonate.

The mass of the **limewater** increases by 0.8 g.

Calculate the mass of **copper oxide** produced. [2 marks]

Because of the law of conservation of mass we know that the total mass of products must be the same as the reactant which is 4.6 g.

One product is carbon dioxide. This went into the limewater so the mass of carbon dioxide produced was 0.8 g.

Therefore, the mass of the copper oxide can be calculated by:

4.6 g – 0.8 g

= 3.8 g   Marks gained: [2 marks]

c They repeat the experiment a further four times.

Their measurements for the decrease in mass of the copper carbonate in grams were:

0.8, 0.5, 0.9, 0.4, 0.6

> **Maths**
> Range = the highest measurement – the lowest measurement

i Calculate the range in measurements. [1 mark]

0.9 – 0.4

= 0.5 (g)   Marks gained:[1 mark]

ii Calculate the percentage uncertainty.

Use the formula: percentage uncertainty = (range/mean) × 100

Give your answer to 1 decimal place.

_____

_____

_____

_____ %   [3 marks]

Relative formula mass

1. What is the relative formula mass, M_r of an oxygen molecule, O_2?

Tick **one** box.

☐ 2   ☐ 16   ☐ 24   ☐ 32   [1 mark]

> **Remember**
> To calculate the relative formula mass, or M_r you add up the relative atomic masses (A_r) of the atoms in the formula.
>
> If these are not given in the exam question, use your copy of the periodic table.

2. Draw **one** line from each molecule diagram to its relative formula mass.

Molecule diagram   **Formula mass**

44

81

18

98

[4 marks]

3. A student carries out a precipitation reaction.

Maths

potassium iodide + lead(II) nitrate $\rightarrow$ lead(II) iodide + potassium nitrate

$$2KI \quad + \quad Pb(NO_3)_2 \quad \rightarrow \quad PbI_2 \quad + \quad 2KNO_3$$

Use the symbol equation to prove that the relative formula mass of reactants is equal to the relative formula mass of the products.

(A_r K = 39; I = 127; Pb = 207; N = 14; O = 16)

_____

_____

_____

_____   [6 marks]

Moles

1. What is the mass of 2 moles of sodium?

Tick **one** box.

☐ 2 g ☐ 22 g ☐ 23 g ☐ 46 g [1 mark]

2. How many moles are in 60 g of calcium?

Tick **one** box.

☐ 1 ☐ 1.5 ☐ 3 ☐ 4.5 [1 mark]

> **Remember**
>
> You can calculate mass of a substance by using the formula:
>
> Mass = moles × relative atomic (A_r) or formula mass (M_r)
>
> This can be rearranged to work out the number of moles:
>
> Moles = mass / relative atomic (A_r) or formula mass (M_r)

3. Calculate the mass in grams of:

a 4 moles of carbon.

_____ [1 mark]

Worked Example

b 5 moles of oxygen (O_2). [4 marks]

The A_r for one oxygen atom is 16.

There are 2 oxygen atoms in each oxygen molecule.

So the M_r of oxygen is 16 × 2 = 32

Mass = moles × M_r [2 marks]

Mass of O_2 = 5 × 32 [1 mark]

Mass of O_2 = 160 g [1 mark]

Marks gained: [4 marks]

c Calculate the number of moles in 283.5 g of hydrogen bromide (HBr). [2 marks]

_____

_____

_____

4. There are 6.02×10^{23} atoms, molecules or ions in a mole of a given substance.

How many molecules are in 1 mole of water? _____

_____ [1 mark]

Amounts of substances in equations

1. 200 g of calcium carbonate is heated to produce calcium oxide and carbon dioxide.

Higher Tier only

The balanced symbol equation for this reaction is:

$$CaCO_3 \rightarrow CaO + CO_2$$

Maths

a Calculate the number of moles of calcium carbonate.

_____

_____

_____ moles   [2 marks]

Maths **b** Calculate the maximum mass of calcium oxide made.

_____

_____

_____ kg   [2 marks]

2. A student carried out the reaction between copper(II) oxide and carbon.

Higher Tier only

The balanced symbol equation for the reaction is:

$$2CuO + C \rightarrow 2Cu + CO_2$$

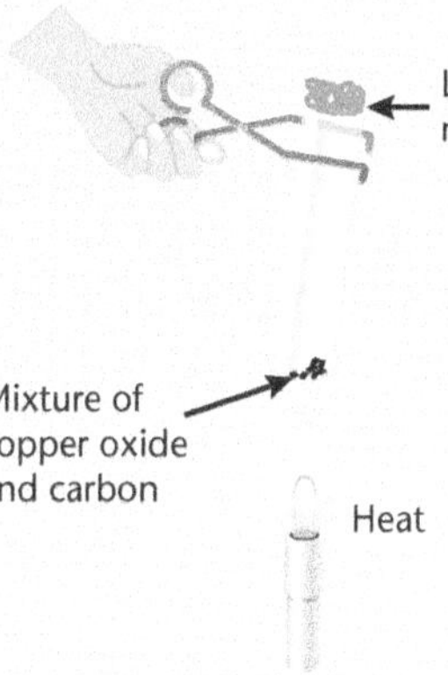

Loose plug of mineral wool

Figure 2 shows the equipment they used.

Practical **a** Suggest the function of the mineral wool.

Mixture of copper oxide and carbon

_____

Heat

_____ [2 marks]

Figure 2

b The student used 1.59 g of copper(II) oxide.

Calculate the expected mass of copper the student should make.

_____

_____

_____

_____ g   [3 marks]

Analyse the question

To answer the question you will need to use the equation mass = moles x relative atomic mass (A_r) or formula mass (M_r) and the chemical symbol equation.

1. Calculate the moles of copper(II) oxide

2. The symbol equation shows that the number of moles of copper(II) oxide = moles of Cu

3. Calculate the mass of copper

Using moles to balance equations

1. How many moles are in 5.5 g of manganese (Mn)?

Higher Tier only

Maths

Tick **one** box

☐ 0.1   ☐ 0.22   ☐ 1   ☐ 2.2   [1 mark]

2. **Figure 3** shows the equipment used to react chlorine with iron.

Higher Tier only

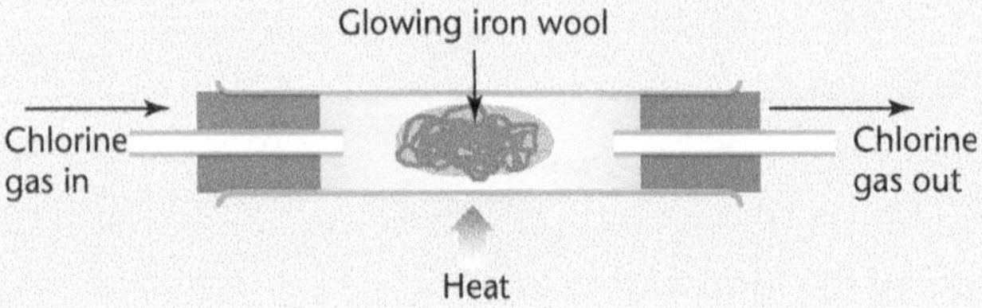

Glowing iron wool

Chlorine gas in →   → Chlorine gas out

Heat

Figure 3

a Write the word equation for this reaction.   [1 mark]

Synoptic

_____

b 1.12 g of iron and 2.13 g of chlorine are used.

Calculate the number of moles of each.

(A_r Fe = 56; A_r Cl = 35.5)

Moles of iron (Fe)

_____

Moles of chlorine (Cl_2)

_____

_____ [2 marks]

Synoptic **c** The product of the reaction is iron(III) chloride, $FeCl_3$.

Use your answers from part **b** to write the balanced symbol equation.

_____

_____ [2 marks]

Limiting reactants

1. Use the words in the box to complete the sentences. [3 marks]

Higher Tier only

chemical	excess	extreme	limiting	physical

In a _____ reaction involving two reactants the

_____ reactant is the one that is all used up by the end
of the reaction.

The reactant in _____ is still
there at the end of the reaction.

2. **Figure 4** shows a piece of potassium in water.

Higher Tier only

Figure 5 shows what is seen at the end of the reaction.

Synoptic

What is the limiting reactant?

Figure 4

Tick **one** box. [1 mark]

☐ Potassium   ☐ Water

☐ Potassium hydroxide   ☐ Hydrogen

3. A scientist carries out a reaction to make copper sulfate crystals.

Higher Tier only

Figure 6 shows the method they used.

Figure 5

a State **one** sign that a chemical reaction
took place.

Practical

Copper oxide

_____

_____
[1 mark]

b Which reactant was in excess?

Explain the reason for your answer.

Sulfuric acid

_____

_____
[2 marks]

| Add copper oxide to sulfuric acid | Filter to remove any unreacted copper oxide | Evaporate to leave behind blue crystals of the 'salt' copper sulfate |

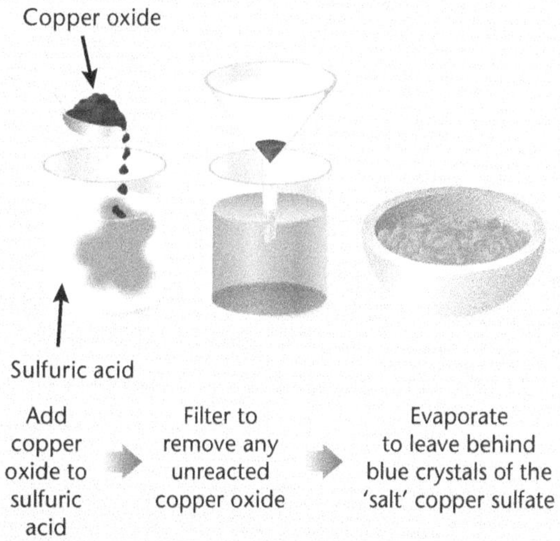

Figure 6

Concentration of solutions

1. How many cm^3 are in 1 dm^3?

Maths Tick **one** box.

- [ ] 10
- [ ] 100
- [ ] 1000
- [ ] 10 000

[1 mark]

2. Which salt solution is the most concentrated?

Tick **one** box

- [ ] 1 g of salt in 2 cm^3 of water
- [ ] 2 g of salt in 10 cm^3 of water
- [ ] 5 g of salt in 20 cm^3 of water
- [ ] 10 g of salt in 25 cm^3 of water   [1 mark]

> **Maths**
>
> The units of concentration show you how to calculate it. If the unit is g/cm^3 then you just need to divide the mass of the solute in g by the volume of the solvent in cm^3. You might have to convert units – for example, from cm^3 to dm^3.
>
> This formula can be rearranged to give you:
>
> mass = volume × concentration
>
> and
>
> volume = mass/concentration

3. Calculate the:

Maths **a** Concentration in **g/cm³** of a solution containing 15 g of copper sulfate in 100 cm^3 of water.

_____ g/cm^3 [1 mark]

b Concentration in **g/dm³** of a solution containing 0.2 g of sodium carbonate in 10 cm^3 of water.

_____ g/dm^3 [2 marks]

c Mass of copper sulfate needed to make 50 cm^3 of a 10g/dm³ solution.

_____ g   [2 marks]

Metal oxides

1. Which reactions are examples of oxidation?

Tick **two** boxes.

☐ sodium carbonate → sodium oxide + carbon dioxide

☐ magnesium + oxygen → magnesium oxide

☐ mercury oxide → mercury + oxygen

☐ zinc + oxygen → zinc(II) oxide [2 marks]

2. Use the words in the box to complete the sentences.

carbonates	oxides	oxidation	reduction	oxates

Metals react with oxygen to produce metal _____.

This reaction is called _____. [2 marks]

3. A student tightly folds a sheet of copper in half.

They heat the copper using a Bunsen burner.

The outside of the copper turns black.

a Complete the word equation for the reaction

copper + oxygen → _____ [1 mark]

Synoptic **b** Balance the symbol equation for the reaction.

$Cu + O_2 → CuO$ [2 marks]

c The student leaves the copper to cool and then unfolds it.

The inside is not black.

Explain why.

_____

_____ [2 marks]

Reactivity series

1. What are the products of the reaction of potassium with water?

Tick **two** boxes.

☐ potassium chloride   ☐ potassium hydroxide

☐ water   ☐ hydrogen   [2 marks]

2. Complete the word equation for the reaction of a metal with sulfuric acid.

_____ + sulfuric acid → magnesium sulfate + _____   [2 marks]

3. A student adds small pieces of metal to water and dilute hydrochloric acid.

Their observations are shown in the table below:

Metal	Reaction with water	Reaction with dilute acid
A	Vigorous fizzing	Very vigorous fizzing
B	Nothing happens	Nothing happens
C	Nothing happens	Vigorous fizzing
D	Nothing happens	Small amount of fizzing

Remember
Less reactive metals do not react with water.

a Put the metals in order of reactivity, the most reactive first.

_____ [2 marks]

b Suggest which metal is copper.

Give a reason for your choice.

_____

_____ [2 marks]

Practical   **c** Explain why the student is not allowed to carry out these tests using sodium.   [2 marks]

Worked Example

To answer this question, consider what you know about sodium and how it reacts.

It is very reactive.   [1 mark]

so it would not be safe   [1 mark]

Marks gained: [2 marks]

Reactivity series – displacement

Figure 1 shows the reactivity series of metals.

Most
Reactive
Sodium
Calcium
Magnesium
Aluminium
Zinc
Iron
Lead
Copper
Gold
Platinum
Least
Reactive

Figure 1

1. Which metal listed in **Figure 1** can be used to displace zinc from zinc sulfate?

Tick **one** box.

☐ Iron ☐ Copper ☐ Magnesium ☐ Gold [1 mark]

2. Complete the displacement reaction word equations using metals from **Figure 1**.

Worked Example

a _____ + sodium → sodium carbonate + _____

[2 marks]

magnesium carbonate + sodium → sodium carbonate + magnesium

Marks gained: [2 marks]

b copper nitrate + _____ → iron nitrate + _____ [2 marks]

3. Study the equations for displacement reactions:

nickel chloride + cobalt → cobalt chloride + nickel

cobalt sulfate + chromium → chromium sulfate + cobalt

Put the metals nickel, cobalt and chromium in order of reactivity, the most reactive first.

Explain how you made your decision.

_____

_____ [3 marks]

Extraction of metals

Use the reactivity series in **Figure 2** to answer questions 1–2.

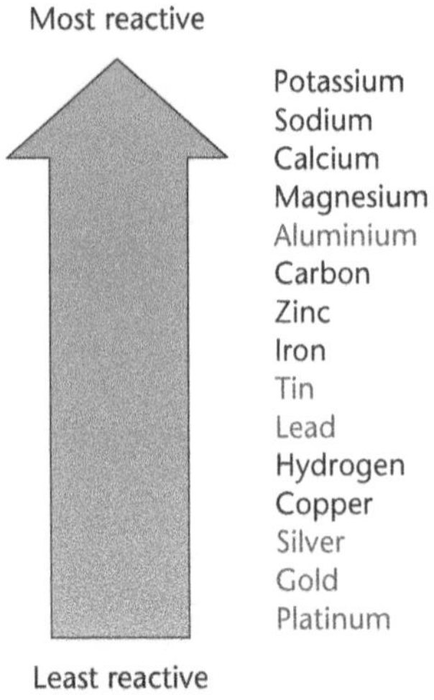

1. How is calcium found in the Earth?

Tick **one** box.

☐ As a mixture, with other metals

☐ As a mixture, with other elements

☐ In a compound, with other elements

☐ As a pure element   [1 mark]

Most reactive

↑

Potassium
Sodium
Calcium
Magnesium
Aluminium
Carbon
Zinc
Iron
Tin
Lead
Hydrogen
Copper
Silver
Gold
Platinum

Least reactive

Figure 2

2. Most metals are extracted from compounds using chemical reactions.

Draw **one** line from each metal to the method of its extraction.

Remember
Only metals less reactive than carbon can be extracted using reduction with carbon.

Metal	Method of extraction
iron	
aluminium	reduction with carbon
sodium	electrolysis
lead	

[4 marks]

3. Zinc is extracted from zinc oxide.

The equation for the reaction is:

zinc oxide + carbon → zinc + carbon dioxide

a Name the substance that is reduced _____ [1 mark]

b Name the substance that is oxidised _____ [1 mark]

c Describe **one** environmental consequence associated with extracting zinc in this way.

_____

_____

_____ [2 marks]

> **Command word**
> You are asked to describe an issue. This means that you will need to discuss the consequence, rather than just name it.

Oxidation and reduction in terms of electrons

1. Which correctly describes what happens during oxidation?

Higher Tier only

Tick **one** box.

☐ A metal gains electrons to form ions.

☐ A metal loses electrons to form ions.

☐ A non-metal gains electrons to form ions.

☐ A non-metal loses electrons to form ions. [1 mark]

> **Remember**
> OILRIG:
> **O**xidation **I**s electron **L**oss
> **R**eduction **I**s electron **G**ain

2. Draw **one** line from each half equation to the type of electron transfer.

Higher Tier only

Half equation	Type of electron transfer
$Na^+ + e^- \rightarrow Na$	
$2Cl^- \rightarrow 2e^- + Cl_2$	Oxidation
$Zn - 2e^- \rightarrow Zn^{2+}$	Reduction
$2F^- - 2e^- \rightarrow F_2$	

[4 marks]

> **Remember**
> The half equation
> $Mg - 2e^- \rightarrow Mg$ can also be written as $Mg \rightarrow Mg^{2+} + 2e^-$

3. Balance the half equation:

Higher Tier only

$2O^{2-} \rightarrow$ _____ $e^- + O_2$ [1 mark]

4. Copper can be extracted from copper oxide by this reaction:

Higher
Tier only

copper oxide + carbon → copper + carbon dioxide

Synoptic

a Complete the balanced symbol equation for this reaction.

_____CuO + _____ → $2Cu$ + _____ [3 marks]

b Which half equation correctly shows reduction in this reaction?

Tick **one** box.

☐ $C^{4-} + 4e^- \rightarrow C$ ☐ $2O^{2-} - 4e^- \rightarrow O_2$

☐ $2Cu^{2+} + 2e^- \rightarrow Cu$ ☐ $Cu \rightarrow Cu^{2+} + 2e^-$ [1 mark]

Reactions of acids with metals

1. Salts can be produced by reacting a metal with an acid.

State the acid and metal you would use to make the salt zinc(II) sulfate.

Metal _____

Acid _____ [2 marks]

2. A student adds magnesium strips to a beaker of hydrochloric acid.

a Complete the word equation for the reaction.

magnesium + hydrochloric acid → _____ + hydrogen [1 mark]

Worked
Example

b Describe **one** sign that the magnesium is reacting with the acid. [1 mark]

There are three signs to choose from:

Bubbles/fizzing from the hydrogen gas that is produced.

Temperature rise because this reaction is exothermic.

The magnesium gets smaller as it reacts to form magnesium
chloride, which dissolves to form a solution.

Marks gained: [1 mark]

Synoptic **c** Describe the test the student can carry out to prove that hydrogen is made.

_____

_____ [3 marks]

d Use the information below to write the balanced symbol equation for this reaction

Magnesium ion = Mg^{2+}

Hydrochloric acid ions = $H^+ Cl^-$

> **Analyse the question**
>
> The charges on the ions will help you to work out the formula of the compounds.
>
> Magnesium chloride has the formula $MgCl_2$ because one magnesium ion needs to join to two chlorine atoms to balance out the charges.

_____ [4 marks]

Neutralisation of acids and making salts

1. Metal oxides are bases.

Which statements are correct about metal oxides?

Tick **two** boxes.

☐ They are soluble. ☐ They are insoluble.

☐ They neutralise alkalis. ☐ They neutralise acids. [2 marks]

2. Name the missing product in the word equation.

potassium hydroxide + hydrochloric acid → _____ + water

[1 mark]

> **Remember**
>
> The second part of the salt's name comes from the acid:
>
> Hydrochloric acid makes chlorides.
>
> Sulfuric acid makes sulfates.
>
> Nitric acid makes nitrates.

3. Draw **one** line from the reactants of a neutralisation reaction to the products.

Worked Example

Reactants

calcium hydroxide + hydrochloric acid
calcium oxide + sulfuric acid
calcium carbonate + sulfuric acid
calcium oxide + nitric acid

Products

calcium sulfate + water + carbon dioxide
calcium chloride + water
calcium sulfate + water
calcium nitrate + water

[4 marks]

49

4. Name the acid and alkali used to produce the salt potassium nitrate.

Acid _____ Alkali _____ [2 marks]

Making soluble salts

1. A student is asked to prepare a pure, dry sample of a soluble salt.

The method they follow is:

A. Gently warm 100 cm³ of sulfuric acid in a beaker using a Bunsen burner.

B. Add a spatula of copper oxide to the acid and stir.

C. Keep adding copper oxide until it is in excess.

D. Remove the excess copper oxide.

E. Crystallise the salt solution.

a State one hazard and way of reducing the risk of harm when carrying out step A.

Hazard: _____

Way of reducing the risk of harm: _____ [2 marks]

b Explain how the student will know when to stop adding copper oxide in step C.

_____ [1 mark]

c Name the salt that is produced.

_____ [1 mark]

d Draw a labelled diagram to show the equipment the student should use for step D.

[2 marks]

e Name this technique _____ [1 mark]

2. They use the equipment in **Figure 3** to carry out step E.

a Label the equipment in **Figure 3** to show the:

– Water bath

– Salt solution [2 marks]

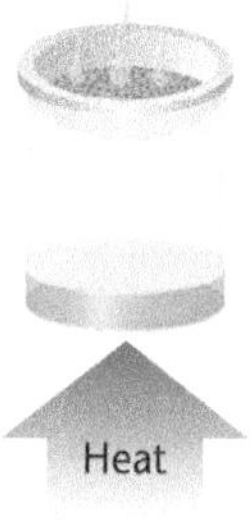

Heat

Figure 3

b Describe how the technique will produce crystals of pure salt.

_____

_____

_____ [2 marks]

pH and neutralisation

1. Which ion do **all** acids contain?

Tick **one** box.

☐ Cl⁻   ☐ SO_4^{2-} ☐ H⁺   ☐ OH⁻   [1 mark]

2. What can be used to measure pH?

Tick **two** boxes.

☐ Litmus solution   ☐ A burette

☐ Universal indicator   ☐ pH probe   [2 marks]

3. Draw **one** line from each pH range to the type of solution.

pH range	Type of solution
1–6	Acidic
7	Alkaline
8–14	Neutral

[3 marks]

4. Complete the equation to show neutralisation.

$H^+ (aq) + $ _____ $(aq) \rightarrow H_2O ($_____$)$ [2 marks]

5. A sodium chloride solution can be produced by adding hydrochloric acid to sodium hydroxide.

a Explain how you could use universal indicator to check when the reaction is **just** complete.

_____

_____

_____

_____ [3 marks]

b State **one** disadvantage of using universal indicator for this technique.

_____

_____ [1 mark]

Strong and weak acids

1. Draw a ring around the correct answer to complete each sentence.

Higher
Tier only

A strong acid

| partially ionises |
| does not ionise |
| fully ionises |

in aqueous solution to produce

| H^+ ions |
| H^- ions |
| OH^- ions |

An example of a strong acid is

| carbonic |
| citric |
| nitric |

acid. [3 marks]

2. Draw **one** line from the particle diagram to the type of acid it represents.

Particle diagram	Type of acid

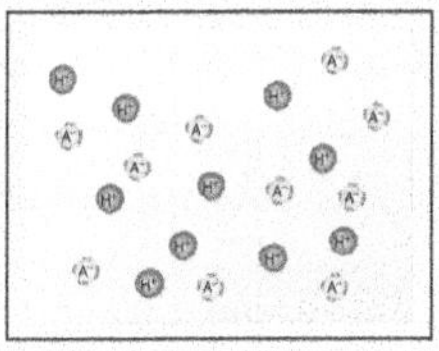

Strong and dilute

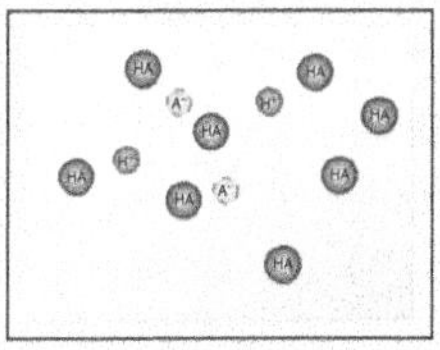

Weak and concentrated

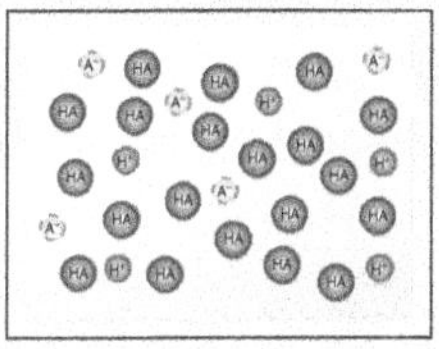

Strong and concentrated

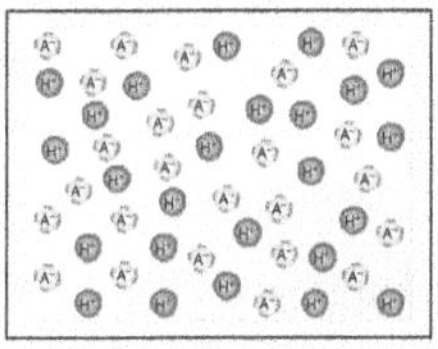

Weak and dilute

[4 marks]

3. The pH scale is related to the concentration of hydrogen ions.

Explain what happens to pH when the concentration of an acid increases.

_____

_____ [2 marks]

The process of electrolysis

1. **Figure 4** shows the equipment used to carry out electrolysis.

a Which letter is pointing to the **cathode**?

Tick **one** box.

A ☐ B ☐ C ☐ D ☐ [1 mark]

b Which letter is pointing to the **electrolyte**?

Tick **one** box.

A ☐   B ☐   C ☐   D ☐   [1 mark]

c Why does the electrolyte need to be molten or in solution?

Tick **one** box.

☐ So the ions are free to move   ☐ So it is inert

☐ To decrease its melting point   ☐ To provide a current

[1 mark]

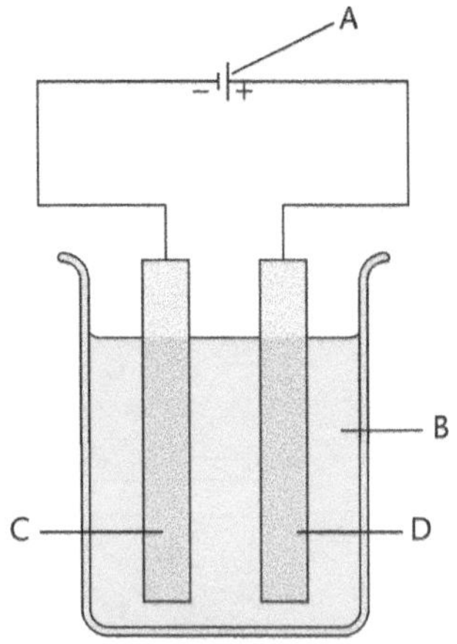

Figure 4

2. Look at **Figure 5**.

Draw **two** arrows on **Figure 5** to show the direction of movement of the ions.   [2 marks]

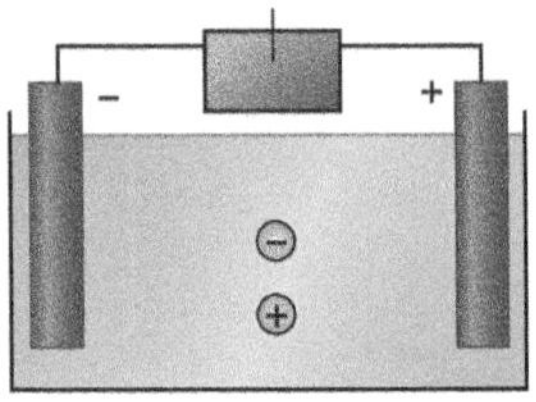

Figure 5

3. Use the words in the box to complete the sentences.

anode	cathode	compounds	electrodes	elements	power supply

During electrolysis ions move to the _____.

Positively charged ions move to the _____.

Negatively charged ions move to the _____.

The ions are discharged as _____.   [4 marks]

Electrolysis of molten ionic compounds

1. Which compounds will conduct electricity **when melted**?

Tick **two** boxes.

☐ Sodium chloride (NaCl)   ☐ Silicon dioxide (SiO_2)

☐ Calcium oxide (CaO)   ☐ Glucose ($C_6H_{12}O_6$)

[2 marks]

Remember

Only ionic compounds will conduct electricity when molten.

Ionic compounds are made up of metals atoms bonded to non-metal atoms.

2. Name the products produced at each electrode when electrolysis is carried out on molten KF.

Anode _____

Cathode _____ [2 marks]

Analyse the question
The question asks you to name the elements. Do not just write the symbols.

3. Look at **Figure 6**.

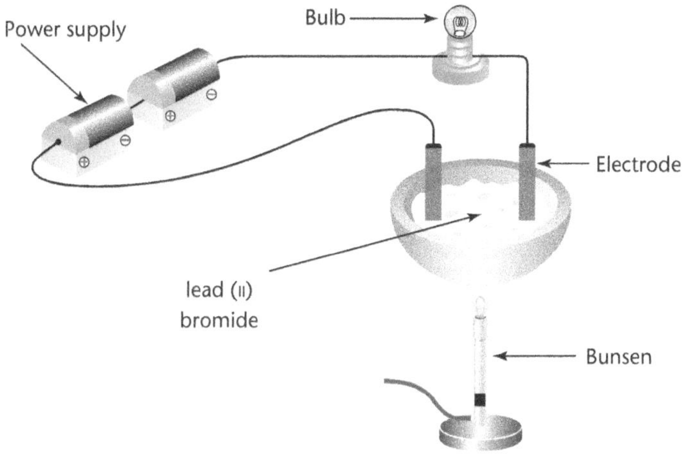

Figure 6

a As the lead(II) bromide is heated it starts to melt.

Explain why the bulb lights.

_____

_____

_____ [3 marks]

b Bubbles of a brown gas are seen at the positive electrode.

Explain why.

_____

_____ [2 marks]

Using electrolysis to extract metals

1. Why are some metals extracted using electrolysis?

Tick **one** box.

- [ ] They are less reactive than carbon.
- [ ] They are more reactive than carbon.
- [ ] They are very unreactive.
- [ ] They are found pure in the Earth's crust. [1 mark]

2. **Figure 7** shows how aluminium is extracted using electrolysis.

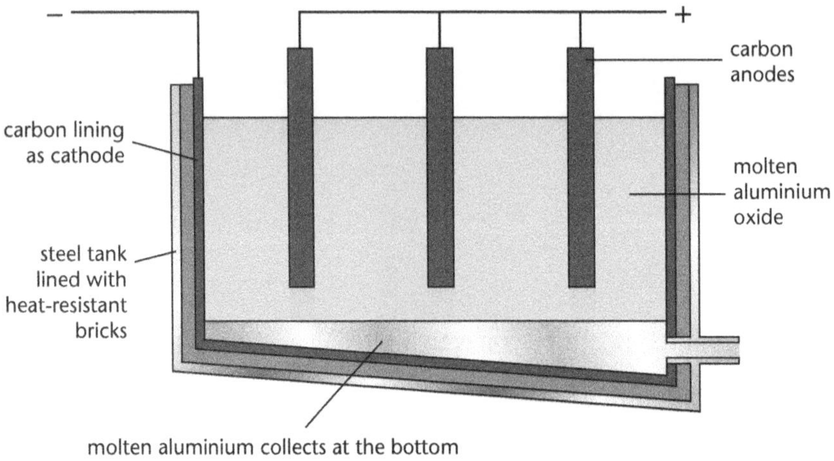

Figure 7

a Explain why aluminium collects at the bottom of the tank.

____

____

____ [2 marks]

b The carbon anodes need to be replaced constantly.

Explain why.

____

____

____ [3 marks]

3.

This information was printed in a magazine.

Literacy

When you throw away aluminium, you are wasting energy.

The processes used to extract aluminium from compounds found in the Earth's crust require a lot of energy.

When aluminium is recycled it is heated to melt it. The molten metal is then used to make new aluminium objects. This process can be repeated again and again.

It requires up to 95% less energy to recycle aluminium than to produce new metal.

Use the information from the magazine and your knowledge and understanding to explain the difference in energy costs between recycling aluminium and extracting new aluminium.

_____

_____

_____

_____

_____

_____

_____

_____ [6 marks]

Electrolysis of aqueous solutions

1. Electrolysis is carried out on copper sulfate ($CuSO_4$) solution.

a Which ions are attracted to the **anode**?

Tick **one** box.

☐	Copper and hydrogen	☐	Oxygen and sulfate
☐	Hydrogen and hydroxide	☐	Sulfate and hydroxide

Remember

Solutions contain water.

Water can split into the ions: hydrogen (H^+) and hydroxide (OH^-)

[1 mark]

b Predict what will be seen at the electrode.

Give a reason for your answer.

Prediction _____

Reason _____ [2 marks]

2. A student is asked to investigate the electrolysis of sodium chloride solution.

Their hypothesis is: hydrogen ions will be discharged at the cathode.

a Describe a method to test the hypothesis. For the method you should include:

- a diagram to show the equipment to use set up correctly

- a way of testing if the hypothesis is correct

_____

_____ [6 marks]

Half equations at electrodes

1. Electrolysis is carried out on melted sodium chloride (NaCl).

Higher Tier only **a** Name the **two** products.

1 _____

2 _____ [2 marks]

2. A, B and C show three different half equations.

Higher Tier only A: $2Br^- - 2e^- \rightarrow Br_2$ B: $2H^+ + 2e^- \rightarrow H_2$ C: $Zn^{2+} + 2e^- \rightarrow Zn$

a Which half equation happens at the anode?

A ☐   B ☐   C ☐   [1 mark]

b Which half equation shows the reduction of a non-metal ion?

A ☐   B ☐   C ☐   [1 mark]

Synoptic **c** Which half equation takes place when electrolysis is carried out on acids?

A ☐   B ☐   C ☐   [1 mark]

3. Use the words in the box to complete the sentences.

Higher Tier only

anode	atoms	cathode	electrons	oxidation	reduction

Positively charged ions are attracted to the _____.

They gain _____.

The reactions are _____. [3 marks]

4. Complete the half equations for the electrolysis of copper sulfate ($CuSO_4$) solution.

Higher Tier only **a** At the cathode: $Cu^{2+} + $ _____ $\rightarrow Cu$ [1 mark]

b At the anode: _____ $-4e^- \rightarrow O_2 + 2H_2O$ [1 mark]

Exothermic and endothermic reactions

1. Use the words in the box to complete the sentences.

exothermic	endothermic	temperature	increases	decreases
energy	created	destroyed	conserved	more	less

Synoptic In a chemical reaction energy is _____. An _____

reaction is one that transfers _____ to the surroundings so that the

temperature of the surroundings _____. The product particles have

_____ energy than the reactant's particles. [5 marks]

2. Which everyday item depends upon an endothermic reaction?

Tick **one** box.

Hand warmers ☐   Self-heating cans ☐

Sports injury packs ☐   Fireworks ☐   [1 mark]

3. The results of Jethro's energy change experiments are listed in Table 1.

Worked Example

Table 1

Sample	Start temperature (°C)	End temperature (°C)	Temperature change (°C)
Ammonium chloride	15	9	−6
Potassium hydroxide	15	30	+13
Ammonium nitrate	15	1	14
Sodium hydroxide	15	32	17

Worked Example **a** Complete Table 1. [2 marks]

Worked Example **b** Which of the solids had the largest exothermic reaction?

Explain your answer. [3 marks]

Comment
To find the temperature change the end temperature is subtracted from the start temperature so the answer for ammonium nitrate should be 1−15 = −14°C. The sign is important because it tells you if the temperature went up or down.

During an exothermic reaction the temperature does go up as heat energy is given out to the surroundings. So all the reactions are exothermic apart from the reaction with ammonium chloride. The reaction with sodium hydroxide is the most exothermic as it has greatest the temperature change.

Marks gained: [3 marks]

Comment
The final answer is correct but an error has been carried through from part **a**. Ammonium nitrate is actually endothermic. If this happened in an exam you would only lose marks for this error in part **a**.

4. Sarah wants to investigate the temperature changes that take place when different metals are added to copper sulfate solution.

Practical

a On the diagram, label the apparatus Sarah will use.

[4 marks]

b Give **two** variables that Sarah should control so the investigation is a fair test.

_____

_____ [2 marks]

What variables must she keep the same?

c Name **two** other pieces of apparatus Sarah will also need.

_____

_____ [2 marks]

How will Sarah measure out the volume of copper sulfate and the mass of metal?

Practical **d** Sarah's results are shown in the table below.

Metal	Temperature (°C)			Mean temperature (°C)
	First test	Second test	Third test	
Magnesium	15.2	4.3	15.8	15.5
Zinc	9.9	9.5	9.6	9.7
Calcium	20.0	20.4	19.9	20.1
Iron	4.1	3.9	4.0	

i One of the results for magnesium is anomalous.

State the anomalous result. _____ [1 mark]

Suggest a reason why it could be anomalous.

_____ [1 mark]

Maths
To find the mean; add up all the results for that metal and then divide by the number of results.

Maths

ii Calculate the mean result for iron and write it in the table. [1 mark]

iii Use the data in the results table to put the metals into order of reactivity.

The first one has been done for you. [2 marks]

iron

Increasing reactivity

Literacy

iv Describe and explain what Sarah could do to improve her results.

_____

_____

_____

_____

_____

_____ [4 marks]

Command
Describe means that you should 'recall' a point and explain means that you should give 'a reason for the point made in the answer'. Marks will only be awarded if the correct reason is given for the point being made.

Reaction profiles

1. For a chemical reaction to occur...

Tick **two** boxes to complete the sentence correctly.

The reacting particles must collide. ☐

The reacting particles must have energy. ☐

The reacting particles bounce off each other. ☐

The reacting particles must have enough
energy to activate the reaction. ☐ [2 marks]

2. **Figure 1** shows the reaction profile for a chemical reaction.

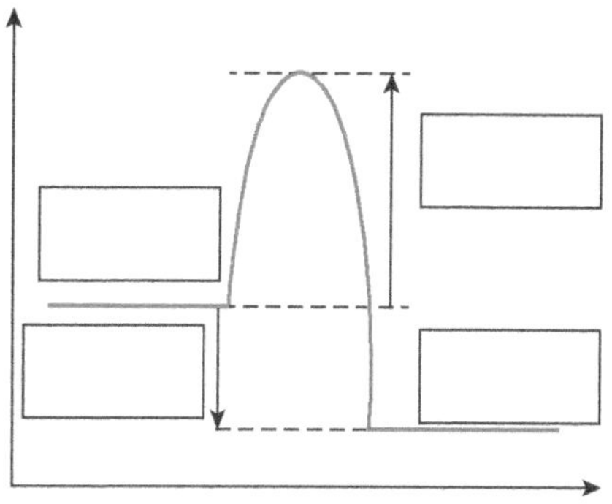

Figure 1

a Add the correct labels to the diagram. [4 marks]

b Describe how you can tell from the diagram that the reaction is exothermic.

_____ [1 mark]

c Explain how the profile would change if the reaction was endothermic.

_____

_____ [2 marks]

Remember
The changes taking place in an endothermic reaction are opposite to those taking place in an exothermic reaction.

3. Jack and John were on a camping trip. They wanted to boil some water using their propane gas stove. Explain what provides the activation energy for the reaction.

Literacy

What do they need to do to light a gas stove?

_____

_____

_____ [3 marks]

Energy change of reactions

1.

Higher
Tier only

Figure 2 shows a reaction profile.

The reaction profile represents the reaction

$$CH_4 + 2O_2 \rightarrow CO_2 + 2H_2O$$

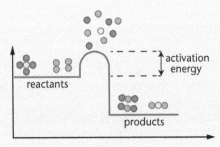

Figure 2

a Describe what happens during the reaction in terms of bond breaking and bond making.

_____

_____

_____ [3 marks]

b Use the bond energies in the table to calculate the overall energy change for the reaction:

$$CH_4 + 2O_2 \rightarrow CO_2 + 2H_2O$$ [5 marks]

Marks gained: [5 marks]

Worked
Example

Bond	C–H	O=O	C=O	H–O
Bond energy (kJ/mol)	412	498	532	465

Work out the bond energies of the reactants.

$4 \times C–H = 4 \times 412 = 1648$

$2 \times O=O = 2 \times 498 = 996$

Total = 1648 + 996 = 2644 kJ/mol   [2 marks for working this out correctly]

Work out the bond energies of the products.

$2 \times C=O = 2 \times 532 = 1064$

$2(2 \times O-H) = 2(2 \times 465) = 2 \times 930 = 1860$

Total $= 1064 + 1860 = 2924$ kJ/mol   [2 marks for working this out correctly]

Now work out the difference between the bond energies of the reactants and products.

$2924 - 2644 = 280$

The difference is 280 kJ/mol. More energy is released than taken in, so the reaction is exothermic.   [1 mark for working this difference out correctly]

c Use the bond energies in the table to determine whether propane, C_3H_8 gives out more or less energy than methane when it burns in air.

$C_3H_8 + 5O_2 \rightarrow 3CO_2 + 4H_2O$

_____

_____

_____

_____

_____

_____   [6 marks]

Bond	C–H	O=O	C=O	H–O	C–C
Bond energy (kJ/mol)	412	498	532	465	346

Follow the method given in the worked example above to work out how much energy is given out when propane burns in air. Then compare your answer to that given in part **b**.

Measuring rates of reaction

1. The time taken for a chemical reaction can be measured in many ways.

Draw a line to match each diagram of the apparatus to the method.   [3 marks]

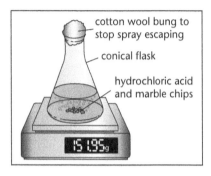

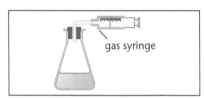

| The volume of gas produced over time |

| The time for a solution to become cloudy |

| The loss of mass over time |

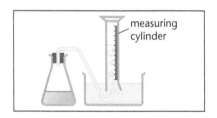

Calculating rates of reaction

1. The rate of a chemical reaction can be found by measuring the quantity of a reactant used or the quantity of product formed over time.

a Write the equation that links the mean rate of reaction with the time taken and the quantity of product formed. [1 mark]

_____

_____

> If you read the question carefully you will find that the answer is hidden there. Highlight the word rate, product and time and then re-write the sentence as an equation. You will not be given this equation in an exam.

b Complete the table of units below.

Quantity of reactant of product measured	Unit of quantity	Unit of rate
Volume		cm³/s
Mass	g	

[2 marks]

Practical **c** Hydrochloric acid was added to calcium metal. In the first 20 seconds, 15 cm³ of gas was collected. Calculate the mean rate of reaction and write the correct units.

_____ [2 marks]

d In the investigation the volume of hydrogen produced was measured every 10 seconds. The results are recorded in the table below.

Time in s	0	10	20	30	40	50
Volume of H_2 in cm³	0	10	15	19	22	22

Use the axes given on the next page to plot a graph of the results. [5 marks]

Mark on the graph where the reaction is:

i fastest   **ii** slowing down   **iii** stopped [3 marks]

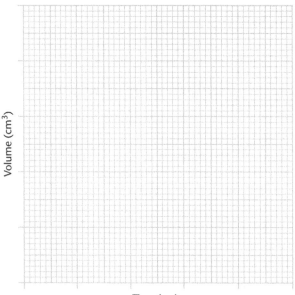

Volume (cm³)

Time (sec)

2. **a** Calculate the rate of reaction from the gradient of the 'blue' graph. [4 marks]

Maths

Choose a straight part of the graph and draw two construction lines (in red).

Worked Example

Measure the value of x and y using the scales
$x = 25, y = 50$

Slope of the gradient $= y/x$ so we divide y by x

$50/25 = 2$

Determine the units using the units given on the axes $x = s$; $y = cm^3$ so the units are cm^3/s

Therefore, rate $= 2$ cm^3/s

Marks gained: [4 marks]

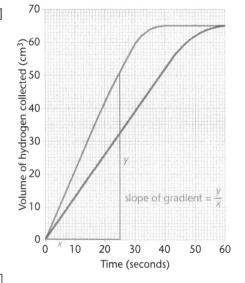

slope of gradient $= \dfrac{y}{x}$

b Calculate the rate of reaction from the gradient of the 'red' graph.

_____ [1 mark]

Effect of concentration and pressure

1. **Figure 1** shows reacting particles, red and blue.

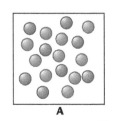
A

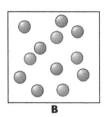
B

Figure 1

a **i** State which diagram shows a low concentration, A or B? _____ [1 mark]

Give a reason for your answer. [1 mark]

_____

ii Predict which reaction will take place at the fastest rate. _____

Give a reason for your answer.

_____ [2 marks]

b If particles A and B are both gases, how could you make the reaction go faster?

Draw a **circle** around the correct answer.

Decrease the pressure, add some water, increase the pressure [1 mark]

2.

Practical

Pramod investigates the reaction between sodium thiosulfate and hydrochloric acid. During the reaction a precipitate of sulfur is produced.

Figure 2 shows a photo of his experiment.

a Pramod wants to measure the rate of reaction.

i What other piece equipment is needed?

_____ [1 mark]

Figure 2

Literacy

ii Describe what he will do. [3 marks]

_____

_____

_____

There are 3 marks here, so you need to write down 3 points in a logical order. Use the information in the diagram to help.

_____

_____

_____

b Pramod thinks that if he increases the concentration of the acid, then the rate of reaction will increase.

> **Remember**
> Don't forget to include the equipment you will use in your answer.

i Describe how he can change the concentration of the acid.

_____

_____ [2 marks]

ii Predict how the time taken for the cross to disappear will change as the concentration of acid increases.

_____ [1 mark]

Effect of surface area

1. Use the words in the box to complete the sentences.

| decrease | increase | particle | collision | kinetic | heat | activation | frequency |

_____ theory explains chemical reactions occur when colliding particles hit or

collide with each other with sufficient energy. The minimum amount of energy is known as

the _____ energy. Increasing the collision _____, means that

there will be more successful collisions per second, which means an _____ in

the rate of reaction. [4 marks]

2. Maria investigated the rate of reaction between calcium carbonate (marble chips) and hydrochloric acid. Maria used the apparatus shown in **Figure 3**.

Maria recorded the mass every 30 seconds. She repeated the experiment using smaller marble chips. She kept the mass the same.

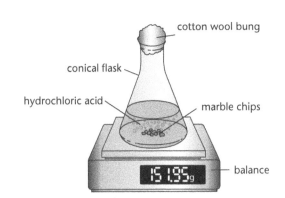

cotton wool bung

conical flask

hydrochloric acid

marble chips

balance

151.95g

Maria plotted her results on a graph.

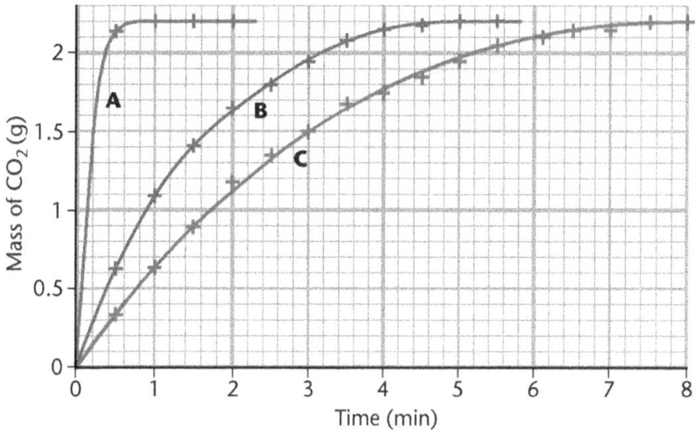

a Why did Maria use the same mass of calcium carbonate in each experiment?

_____ [1 mark]

b Match the letter of the graph to the size of particle used.

___ powder calcium carbonate

___ single chip of calcium carbonate

___ small chips of calcium carbonate [3 marks]

c Look at the graph above and write down the amount of CO_2 lost after 2 minutes. Give your answers to 2 decimal places.

i Powdered calcium carbonate. _____

ii A single chip of calcium carbonate. _____ [2 marks]

d State **one** conclusion she can make about the effect of surface area on rate of reaction.

_____ [1 mark]

e Explain why the same mass of CO_2 was produced in each experiment.

_____

_____ [2 marks]

Effect of temperature

1. Which of the following statements are false?

Tick **two** boxes.

Increasing the temperature decreases the rate of reaction. ☐

Increasing the temperature increases the rate of reaction. ☐

Increasing the temperature increases the kinetic energy of the reacting particles. ☐

Increasing the temperature increases the potential energy of the reacting particles. ☐ [2 marks]

2. A student collected some data and recorded it in the table below.

Time in seconds	Volume of gas in cm³ collected at Temperature, T1	Volume of gas in cm³ collected at Temperature, T2
0	0	0
10	12	31
20	23	50
30	34	63
40	34	64
50	63	64
60	63	64

a State the anomaly in the data collected at T1. _____ [1 mark]

b Suggest what the student should do about this data point.

_____ [1 mark]

c Which set of data was collected at the highest temperature?

Give a reason for your answer.

_____

_____ [2 marks]

Maths

d Calculate the mean rate of reaction for T1.

Give your answer to 3 significant figures.

_____

_____

> **Maths**
> You will need to remember this equation; to get the units right, put them into the equation as well.

_____ [3 marks]

e Describe how the rate of reaction changes throughout the reaction.

_____

_____ [2 marks]

Effect of catalyst

1. Use the words in the box to complete the sentences.

| particle | collision | catalysts | specific | limited | excess | speed | used |

_____ are substances that change the _____ of a chemical

reaction but are not _____ up in the reaction. They are used in small amounts

and are _____ to one single reaction.   [4 marks]

2. Hydrogen peroxide decomposes to produce water and oxygen gas.

a Complete the equation for the reaction.

hydrogen peroxide → _____ + _____   [1 mark]

b Explain why Joe and Mohammad want to find a catalyst for the reaction.

Suggest a suitable method they could use to find the best catalyst.

> Use your knowledge and understanding of both practical chemistry and catalysts to answer this question.

_____

_____

_____

_____

_____

_____

_____

_____   [6 marks]

c The results are shown in the table below.

Experiment	Substance added	Time to collect gas (s)
1	No substance	100
2	Potato	50
3	Manganese oxide	10
4	Iron oxide	20

i Why did they not add anything in experiment 1?

_____ [1 mark]

ii Which substance was the best catalyst for this reaction? What information leads you to this conclusion?

_____

_____ [2 marks]

iii The graph in **Figure 4** shows the reaction profile for the reaction.

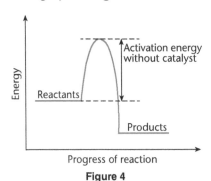

Figure 4

Draw a line on the graph to show how the reaction profile changes when a catalyst is used. [1 mark]

Reversible reactions and energy changes

1. In some chemical reactions, the products of the reactions can react to produce the original reactants.

ammonium chloride ⇌ ammonia + hydrogen chloride

a Write the forwards reaction.

_____ [1 mark]

b Write the backwards reaction.

_____ [1 mark]

c What does the ⇌ symbol mean?

_____ [1 mark]

d Describe how you change the direction of the reaction.

_____ [2 marks]

> Look at the words written on the equation. There is a mark for each condition.

e Write a balanced symbol equation for the reaction. Include the state symbols.

_____ [3 marks]

2. Asaf heated some blue copper sulfate crystals and they went white.

Practical **a** If the reaction is reversible, predict what will happen when he adds water.

_____ [1 mark]

b He notices that copper sulfate gets hot during the reverse reaction. What does this tell him about the type of reaction taking place?

_____ [1 mark]

c From his observations, describe the energy changes that occur during the forwards reaction.

_____

_____ [2 marks]

Equilibrium and Le Chatelier's Principle

1. Use the words in the box to complete the sentences.

Synoptic

| time | open | closed | speed | rate | reversible | irreversible | equilibrium |

When a _____ reaction occurs in a _____ system,

_____ is reached when the forward and reverse reactions occur at

exactly the same _____. [4 marks]

2. A fizzy drink contains carbon dioxide.

$$CO_2(g) \rightleftharpoons CO_2(aq)$$

Literacy Explain why the carbon dioxide gas is in equilibrium with the dissolved carbon dioxide when it is in the closed bottle, but not when it is in a glass.

_____

_____

_____

_____

Start this question by noting down the difference between a closed bottle and an open glass. Then look at the equation and describe what will happen in each case.

_____ [4 marks]

3. What can Le Chatelier's Principle be used to predict?

Higher Tier only

Tick **two** boxes.

If a substance is a catalyst ☐

Effects of changing the temperature on a system ☐

Effects of changing the pressure on a system ☐

If the system is at equilibrium ☐ [2 marks]

4. Le Chatelier's Principle is applied to the following reaction:

$$A + B \rightleftharpoons C$$

Describe what will happen if the concentration of C increases.

_____

You will need to learn Le Chatelier's Principle and be able to apply it to different situations.

_____ [2 marks]

Changing the position of equilibrium

1. The Haber Process produces ammonia from nitrogen and hydrogen. The reaction is exothermic.

Higher Tier only

a Balance the equation:

_____N_2 (g) + _____H_2 (g) $\rightleftharpoons$ _____NH_3 (g)   [2 marks]

In the reactor, the nitrogen and hydrogen are heated at high pressures and passed over a catalyst.

b Changing the reaction conditions will alter the position of the equilibrium.

Draw lines to match each action to the description of how the equilibrium will move.

Increasing the pressure   no change to position of equilibrium

Changing the catalyst   equilibrium moves to the left

Increasing the temperature   equilibrium moves to the right   [3 marks]

2. During the Contact Process, sulfur dioxide is converted to sulfur trioxide.

a Balance the equation:

_____SO_2 (g) + O_2 (g) $\rightleftharpoons$ _____SO_3(g)   [2 marks]

The graph in **Figure 5** shows how the amount of sulfur trioxide produced varies with temperature.

b State which gas would need be removed to produce more SO_3.

_____   [1 mark]

c Predict what will happen to the position of equilibrium when the pressure is reduced. Give a reason for your answer.

Count the number of particles on each side of the reaction.

_____

_____ [2 marks]

d What conclusion can you draw from this graph?

_____ [1 mark]

Suggest a reason for your answer.

_____

_____ [2 marks]

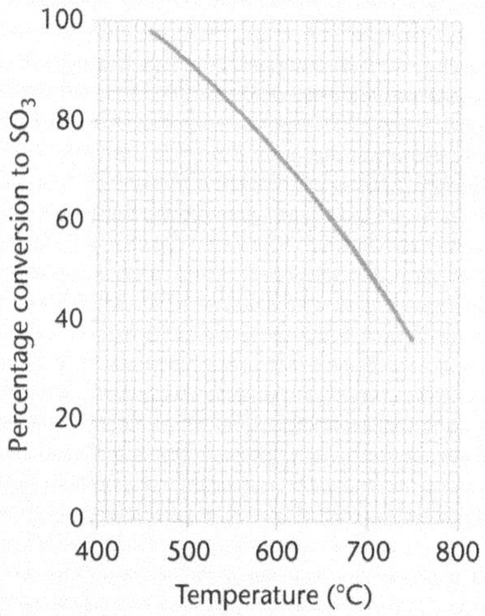

Figure 5

(Graph: x-axis "Temperature (°C)" from 400 to 800; y-axis "Percentage conversion to SO$_3$" from 0 to 100.)

Crude oil and hydrocarbons

1. Use the correct word from the box to complete the sentences.

Synoptic

| renewable | finite | plants | marine | animals | plankton | biomass |

Crude oil is a _____resource found in rocks. It was made from the remains

of _____ and other ancient _____ compressed in mud over

millions of years. [3 marks]

2. Crude oil is a fossil fuel, which of the following are also fossil fuels?

Tick **two** boxes.

Coal ☐   Geothermal power ☐   Natural gas ☐   Solar power ☐   [2 marks]

Structure and formulae of alkanes

1. Use the correct word from the box to complete the sentences.

Synoptic

| one | two | three | four | single | double | triple | family | homologous |

Alkanes all belong to the same _____ series. All the bonds in alkanes are

_____. Each carbon atom forms _____ bonds. Hydrogen

can form _____ bond; so four hydrogen atoms bond to one carbon

atom to make a methane molecule. [4 marks]

2. Molecules can be represented in different ways.
Look at **Figure 1**.

Write down the formula of this molecule.

$$H-\underset{\underset{H}{|}}{\overset{\overset{H}{|}}{C}}-H$$

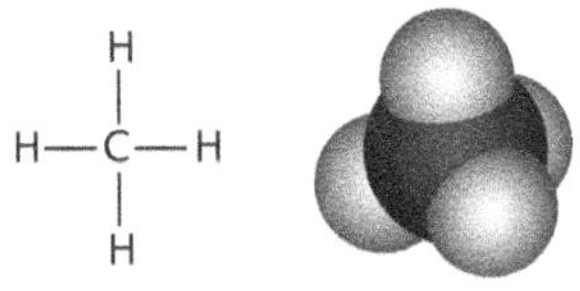

Figure 1

_____ [1 mark]

3. Complete the table below. The first row has been done for you.

Name	Number of carbon atoms	Formula	Displayed formula
Methane	1	CH_4	H—C—H with H above and H below
	2	C_2H_6	
Propane		C_3H_8	
	4		H—C—C—C—C—H with H atoms above and below each C

[3 marks]

4. The general formula for the alkanes is C_nH_{2n+2} where n is the number of carbon atoms.

Write down the formula for:

i an alkane containing 5 carbon atoms _____

ii an alkane containing 8 carbon atoms _____

[2 marks]

> Here you need to substitute the numbers into the formula. 2n+2 means (2 × number of carbon atoms in the molecule) + 2

Fractional distillation and petrochemicals

1. Are the following statements true or false?

Tick the **correct** box.

A polymer is an example of a petrochemical   true ☐   false ☐

All fossil fuels come from crude oil   true ☐   false ☐ [2 marks]

2. Which of these mixtures show formulae of substances that could be in the gaseous fraction of crude oil?

Tick **one** box.

C_2H_4, C_2H_5OH, $C_6H_{10}O$ ☐ C_2H_6, C_3H_8, C_4H_{10} ☐

C_2H_4, $C_2H_5CO_2H$, C_4H_8 ☐ C_2H_6, C_2H_5Br, C_2H_7O ☐   [1 mark]

3. A fractional distillation column is shown in **Figure 2**.

Label the diagram to show where the following fractions are collected.

a bitumen

b diesel

c liquefied petroleum gas (LPG)

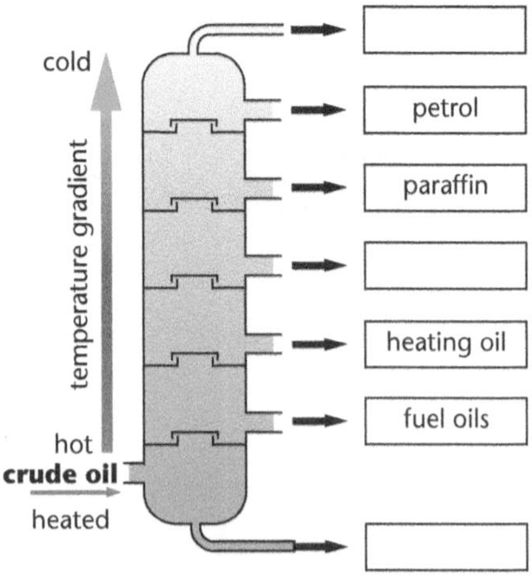

_____

_____ [2 marks]

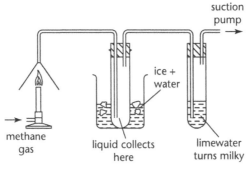

Figure 2

Literacy **d** Explain why fuel oils are collected near the bottom of the column whereas petrol is collected near the top of the column.

_____

_____

_____

_____ [3 marks]

> To get full marks you will need to compare the two molecules with each other, making three points. A good place to start is to think about the relative size of the molecules.

Combustion of fuels

1. John wants to find out which new substances are made when methane, a hydrocarbon, burns in air. He sets up the apparatus shown in **Figure 3**.

Practical

Figure 3

a State the name of the gas in the air that reacts with methane. _____

[1 mark]

b State the name of the gas that turns limewater milky. _____ [1 mark]

c State the name of the liquid collected. _____ [1 mark]

d During the experiment, John noticed a black substance appearing on the funnel.

Suggest a reason for this.

_____

_____ [2 marks]

e Write a word equation for the reaction taking place in the experiment:

methane + oxygen → _____ + _____ [1 mark]

f Balance the symbol equation:

$CH_4 +$ _____$O_2 \rightarrow CO_2 +$ _____H_2O [1 mark]

Cracking and alkenes

1. Kerosene was cracked in the lab using the following equipment. This produced a mixture of products including ethene.

Practical

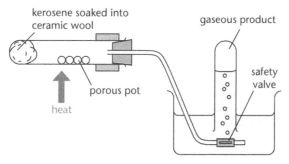

kerosene soaked into ceramic wool

gaseous product

safety valve

porous pot

heat

a In this experiment, state the name of the catalyst. _____ [1 mark]

b Explain why it is important to get the catalyst really hot before heating the kerosene.

_____ [1 mark]

c During the experiment three test tubes of gas were collected. Bromine water was added to each tube to see if an alkene had been made.

i Describe the colour change would you expect to see if an alkene is present.

_____ [1 mark]

ii The first test showed a negative result for alkenes but the second and third showed a positive result. Suggest a reason for these observations.

_____

_____ [2 marks]

iii A student then decided to carry out the bromine test of the starting reactant. Predict the result.

_____ [1 mark]

2.

Literacy

Industrial cracking plants are often built near oil refineries. Use the data in the table below to suggest a reason why.

Product	Supply in tonnes	Demand in tonnes
Petrol	100	300
Diesel	200	100
Kerosene	250	50

Use the information in the table to help structure your ideas.

_____

_____

_____

_____ [4 marks]

Pure substances, mixtures and formulations

1. Substances can be pure or they can be mixtures. Which of these is a mixture?

Tick **one** box.

Potassium ☐   Bromine ☐

Potassium bromide ☐   Potassium bromide solution ☐   [1 mark]

2. Look at the boxes on the right.

Which box or boxes contain:

a   One element? _____

b   A pure substance? _____

c   A mixture of an element and compound?

_____   [4 marks]

3. Mixtures can be separated by physical processes.

The table below shows some mixtures to be separated and possible methods of separation.

Tick **one** box in each row to show the best method of separation for each mixture.

Substance to separate	Method of separation			
	Filtration	Crystallisation	Simple distillation	Fractional distillation
Petrol from crude oil				
Magnesium sulfate crystals from magnesium sulfate solution				
Sand from a mixture of sandy sea water				

[3 marks]

Chromatography and R_f values

1.

Practical

Paper chromatography can be used to separate a mixture of dyes.

A spot of the mixture was placed on some chromatography paper and placed into a chromatography tank as shown in **Figure 1**.

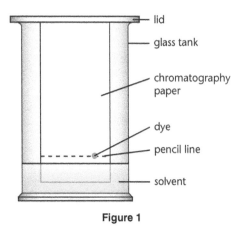

Figure 1

a Suggest a reason why the start line is drawn in pencil rather than ink.

_____ [1 mark]

b Suggest a reason why the solvent level is below the pencil line.

_____ [1 mark]

c After about 40 minutes the chromatography paper was taken out of the tank and dried. **Figure 2** shows what it looked like.

i How many different dyes were in the mixture? _____ [1 mark]

ii Explain what happened during the experiment.

_____

_____

_____

_____

Figure 2

[3 marks]

2.

A student used chromatography to investigate the components of a food dye. The resulting chromatogram is shown in **Figure 3**.

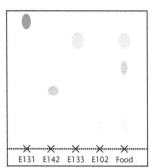

E131 E142 E133 E102 Food

Figure 3

a Why has the student included some standard colours in the experiment? [1 mark]

So he can compare the results and hopefully identify the components.

Marks gained: [1 mark]

Comment
Standard colours are labelled by E numbers. They are pure compounds and so the chromatogram will always only have one spot.

b Write down the identified components in the mixture. [2 marks]

E102 (yellow spot) **[1 mark]** E142 (green spot) **[0 marks]**, E133 (light blue spot)

Marks gained: [2 marks]

Comment
E142 is incorrect; the others are correct. If you look carefully at the chromatogram, you will see that the green spots occur at different levels on the paper. This means that they are different substances. When answering a question, always look at the number of marks. In this question, 2 marks could suggest that there are only two correct answers.

c How can the student identify which green colour is in the food? [2 marks]

Repeat the experiment using different standards with green colours and hope that he finds a match. Or he could work out the R_f value and look it up in a reference table.

Marks gained: [2 marks]

Comment
You will need to learn this equation because it may not always be given to you. Always show your working because if you make a mistake you may still get some of the marks. This final answer is incorrect as it has not been given to 2 significant figures. You would lose a mark for this in the exam. The correct answer is 0.77. The second 6 is rounded up to 7 because the value that follows it is greater than 5.

d The green spot has moved 9.5 cm and the solvent front had moved 12.4 cm

Calculate the R_f value of the green spot, giving your answer to 2 significant figures. [2 marks]

Comment
When using reference tables make sure they have used the same solvent otherwise you will get the answer wrong.

$$R_f \text{ value} = \frac{\text{distance travelled by a dye}}{\text{distance travelled by solvent front}}$$

$R_f = 9.5/12.4 = 0.766129032$

Marks gained: [2 marks]

e How could the student use this value to identify the green colour? [1 mark]

Look up the R_f value in a reference book or website.

Marks gained: [1 mark]

Tests for common gases

1. Draw a line to match each gas with its test.

| Hydrogen |
| Oxygen |
| Carbon dioxide |
| Chlorine |

| Relights a glowing splint |
| Bleaches damp litmus paper white |
| Burns rapidly with a 'pop' sound |
| Turns limewater milky |

[4 marks]

2.

Practical

Simon is investigating the reaction between calcium carbonate (marble chips) and hydrochloric acid using the equipment in **Figure 4**.

He notices a gas being given off and wants to identify it. He must collect some gas to test.

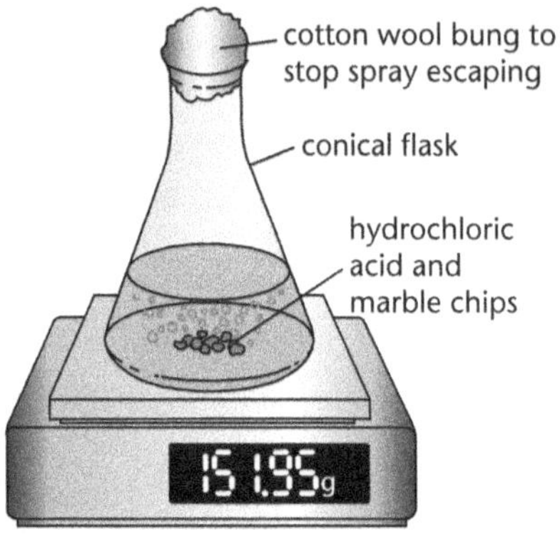

cotton wool bung to stop spray escaping

conical flask

hydrochloric acid and marble chips

151.95g

Figure 4

Literacy **a** Explain how he could modify the equipment to collect the gas, using the words in the box.

| delivery tube   water trough   boiling tube   bung |

_____

_____

_____

_____ [4 marks]

b When a glowing splint was put into a tube of gas, it went out.

What conclusion can the student make from this test?

_____ [1 mark]

c When some limewater was put into the tube of gas, it went milky.

What conclusion can the student make from this test?

_____ [1 mark]

d What could the student do to make sure his result was correct?

_____ [1 mark]

The Earth's atmosphere – now and in the past

1. Today's atmosphere mainly contains nitrogen and oxygen.

Approximately 1% of the atmosphere is made up of other gases.

Which gas is not found in today's atmosphere?

Tick **one** box.

Carbon dioxide ☐   Ammonia ☐   Water vapour ☐   Argon ☐   [1 mark]

2. **a** Suggest a reason why there are several different theories about the early atmosphere.

_____ [1 mark]

b Some scientists think that the early atmosphere on Earth was similar to that on Mars today. The bar chart in **Figure 1** shows the composition of the atmosphere on Mars.

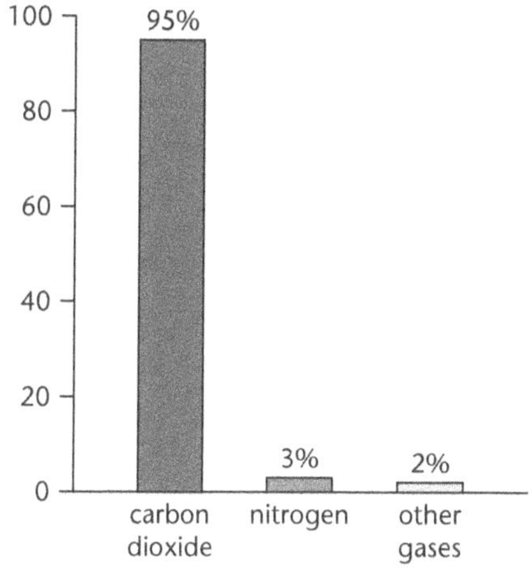

Figure 1

Maths

What is the ratio of the amount of carbon dioxide gas on Mars to nitrogen and the other gases present?

[2 marks]

Maths

First write the percentage as a fraction; then divide the fractions by the smallest number; write down the ratio. Remember to show your working; you may get some marks even if the final answer is wrong.

_____

_____

c Explain why planets such as Mars are used as a model for the early atmosphere on Earth.

_____

_____ [1 mark]

Changes in oxygen and carbon dioxide

1.

Synoptic

a Complete the sentence using the correct word from the box.

| respiration | photosynthesis | degassing |

[1 mark]

Algae and plants produced the oxygen that is now in the atmosphere by the process

of _____.

b Complete the word equation for the reaction.

_____ + water $\xrightarrow{\text{light}}$ _____ + oxygen   [2 marks]

c Explain what happened to the carbon dioxide and oxygen levels in the atmosphere as more plants evolved.

> Look at the equation in part **b** – reactants are used up but products are made.

_____

_____ [2 marks]

d One theory suggests that the oxygen produced by algae was removed by the oxidation of iron.

If this theory is correct, suggest a reason why oxygen levels in the early atmosphere started to increase.

_____

_____ [2 marks]

2. Carbon dioxide was also decreased by the formation of limestone and fossil fuels that contain carbon. Read through the statements below about the formation of crude oil.

Number the statements in the correct order.

The first one has been done for you.

Sea creatures and plants in plankton died about 150 million years ago. [1]

Pressure and temperature increased. [ ]

They didn't decay properly due to a lack of oxygen. [ ]

Crude oil was formed. [ ]

They were buried under layers of silt in the sand. [ ]   [2 marks]

Greenhouse gases

1. Which gas is not a greenhouse gas?

Tick **one** box.

Carbon dioxide ☐   Methane ☐   Water vapour ☐   Oxygen ☐   [1 mark]

2. **a** Label the diagram to show how the greenhouse effect works.

The Sun heats up the Earth

The Earth radiates some energy back into space

Greenhouse gases trap heat

[2 marks]

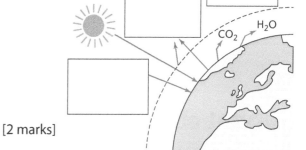

b Describe the wavelength of solar radiation and the wavelength of radiation radiated back from the Earth.

_____

_____ [2 marks]

c Why is the greenhouse effect important to life on Earth?

_____ [1 mark]

3. The graph shows the concentration of carbon dioxide in the atmosphere above Hawaii from 2000 to 2014.

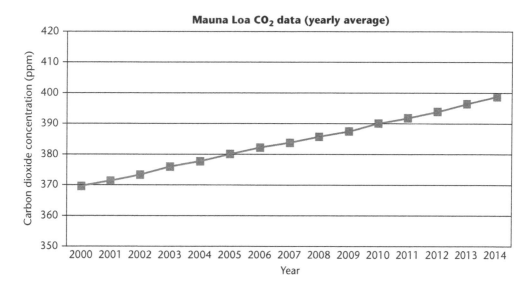

a What does ppm mean? _____ [1 mark]

b **i** Use the graph to calculate the increase in CO_2 from 2000 to 2010.

_____ [2 marks]

Maths **ii** If the amount of CO_2 continues to increase at the same rate, predict what the concentration of CO_2 will be in 2020.

_____ [1 mark]

> Expand the *x*-axis to 2020 and expand the graph or use your answer to part **i** and do a calculation.

c Describe **two** human activities that may have caused this increase in CO_2 levels.

_____

_____ [2 marks]

Global climate change

1. An increase in global temperatures will cause climate change.

What is one possible effect of climate change?

Tick **one** box.

Global dimming ☐   Respiratory problems in humans ☐

More frequent and severe storms ☐   Deforestation ☐   [1 mark]

2. If global warming continues there will be big changes in the environment.

a Draw a line to match the environmental change with its possible impact.

Environmental change

| Temperature stress for humans and wildlife |

| Water stress for humans and wildlife |

| Changes to food production capacity |

| Changes to distribution of wildlife |

Possible impact

| Migration patterns change |

| Changes in agriculture i.e. what crops will grow |

| It will be too hot to make a living |

| No fresh water supplies in some areas |

[4 marks]

Literacy **b** Describe some possible consequences for people living in areas affected by climate change.

> Here you need to put forward ideas and discuss the risks that people will face. Try to make 3 points here – one for each mark.

_____

_____

_____ [3 marks]

Carbon footprint and its reduction

1. Complete the sentence using words in the box.

Synoptic

| polluting | monoxide | greenhouse | dioxide | handprint | footprint |

The carbon _____ is the total amount of carbon _____

and other _____ gases emitted over the full life cycle of a product,

service or event. [3 marks]

2. **a** Which of the following actions will decrease our carbon footprint at home?

Tick **two** boxes.

Double glazed window ☐

Playing loud music in every room at the same time ☐

Oil central heating ☐

Cavity wall insulation ☐

Turning up the heating in winter ☐ [2 marks]

Literacy **b** Explain why it is important for us all to reduce our carbon footprints and suggest a reason why it is sometimes hard to do it. [4 marks]

Worked Example

If everyone does their bit then the levels of greenhouse gases released into the atmosphere will start to decrease or at least not increase further. [**1 mark**] This will help to reduce the effects of global warming. [**1 mark**]

Reducing your carbon footprint can be expensive e.g. it costs a lot of money to install solar panels with solar cells in your home. [**1 mark**] It can mean you have to think carefully about what you wear. For example, wearing a fleece inside means that you can turn down the heating. [**1 mark**] This is a lifestyle change.

Marks gained: [4 marks]

Air pollution from burning fuels

1. Many of the pollutants found in the atmosphere come from burning fuels.

Use the words in the box to describe where each of the pollutants come from.

power stations	fossil fuels	combustion engines
burning	incomplete combustion	coal

a Carbon dioxide – _____ _____ in _____

or _____ [1 mark]

b Carbon particulates – _____ of _____ or other

_____ [1 mark]

c Sulfur dioxide – _____ _____ in _____

and _____ [1 mark]

d Nitrogen monoxide – results from high temperatures in _____ [1 mark]

2. The level of carbon monoxide in the atmosphere is carefully monitored. Look at the data in the table.

Worked Example

Time of day	2.00 pm	4.00 pm	6.00 pm	8.00 pm	10.00 pm
CO (ppm) in a city centre	5.0	5.2	5.9	5.6	5.0
CO (ppm) in the countryside	1.0	0.0	1.1	1.0	0.9

a Describe what the data shows about the levels of carbon monoxide. [2 marks]

There is always more CO present in the city centre that in the countryside. [1 mark]

The level of CO peaks at 6.00 pm in the city but in the countryside is pretty constant. [1 mark]

Marks gained: [2 marks]

Comment

These are not the only correct answers. As long as the answer is supported by data in the table it will be accepted.

b Suggest a reason for your answer to part **a**. [2 marks]

There are more cars/vehicles in the city centre than the countryside, especially during rush hour (approx. 6pm). [1 mark]

CO is produced by the incomplete combustion of petrol/diesel engines. [1 mark]

Marks gained: [2 marks]

Comment

It is important here to make sure that your answers are linked to the ideas you gave in part **a** otherwise it will be marked wrong.

What does the Earth provide for us?

1. Complete the sentences by using the words from the box.

environment	finite	non-renewable	renewable

A _____ resource is one that can be replaced as quickly as it is used.

A _____ resource is one that cannot be made again. Sustainable

development is about meeting people's present needs without spoiling the

_____ for the future. [3 marks]

2. Which of the following is a sustainable resource? Tick **one** box.

Crude oil ☐   Iron ore ☐   Managed forest ☐   Coal ☐   [1 mark]

3. Today, many traditional materials are being replaced by synthetic ones.
Complete the table by using the words in the box.

iron	paper	PVC	carbon fibres	nylon	polystyrene

Object	Traditional material	Synthetic material
Window frames	Wood	
Disposable cup	Paper	
Blouse	Cotton	
Disposable bag		Poly(ethene)

[4 marks]

4. Two students are concerned about using resources wisely. They discuss whether to
make a new object from wood from a managed forest or plastic from crude oil.

What advice would you give them?

> Start by comparing the two materials. Write down the advantages and disadvantages of each one. Then state, giving your reasons, which you would choose.

_____

_____

_____

_____

_____ [4 marks]

Safe drinking water

1. In many developed countries fresh water is supplied from reservoirs.

Practical **a** In some countries drinking water is made from sea water because they do not have a supply of fresh water. The simple distillation apparatus in **Figure 1** can be used to distil a sample of salt water.

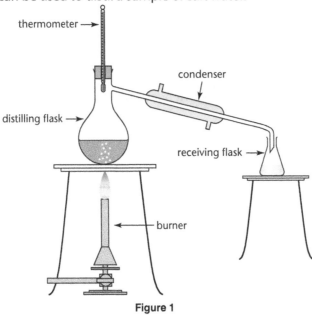

thermometer →

condenser

distilling flask →

receiving flask →

burner

Figure 1

Label the following:

i salt water **ii** pure water [1 mark]

b Describe how distillation works.

_____

_____

_____ [2 marks]

c How could the water be tested to show it is pure?

_____

_____ [2 marks]

d Explain why desalination of salty or sea water is expensive.

_____ [1 mark]

Waste water treatment

1. There is no new water on the planet. Water is continuously recycled via the water cycle. **Figure 2** shows a diagram of the water cycle.

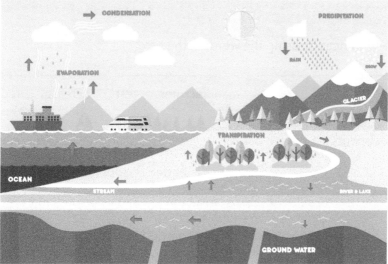

Figure 2

a Describe how a particle of water is continuously recycled.

> Look at Figure 2 to help you describe how water can move. Don't forget to use scientific terms.

_____

_____

_____ [3 marks]

b State why it is important to treat waste water.

_____ [1 mark]

2. **a** Complete the sentences by using the words in the box.

| diseases | organic | microbes | chemicals | sewage | inorganic |

_____ and agricultural waste water require the removal of

_____ matter and harmful _____.

Industrial waste may require the removal of organic matter and harmful

_____. [4 marks]

b Describe **one** possible effect of not treating agricultural waste water.

_____ [1 mark]

95

Describe **one** possible effect of not treating industrial waste.

_____ [1 mark]

Life cycle assessment (LCA)

1.

a Complete the sentences by using the words in the box.

| industry   products   assess   manufactures   test   increase   reduction |

Life cycle assessments are carried out to _____ the environmental

impact of _____. They may be used to encourage a

_____ in waste and raise awareness of environmental impact.   [3 marks]

b All babies need nappies. To help parents choose whether to use disposal nappies made from cellulose fibres, a super-absorbent polymer, or reusable cloth nappies, an LCA is available. The table below shows some data comparing disposable to reusable nappies.

Impact (per baby, per year)	Disposable nappies	Reusable nappies
Energy needed to produce the product	8900 MJ	2532 MJ
Waste water	28 m³	12.4 m³
Raw materials used	596 kg	29 kg
Domestic solid waste produced	361 kg	4 kg

i Look at the information in the table

Explain which type of nappy is better for the environment. You must give reasons for your answer.

_____

_____

_____

_____ [3 marks]

ii Describe what may happen to each nappy at the end of its useful life.

_____

_____ [2 marks]

c State a reason why it is important to identify the source behind a life cycle assessment.

_____ [1 mark]

Ways of reducing the use of resources

1. Draw a line to match each word with its meaning.

Reduce	Methods for making new materials from ones that have already been used
Reuse	Use less to avoid waste
Recycle	Use the object again instead of throwing it away

[3 marks]

2. The table below shows some information about aluminium and tin.

Metal	Amount in Earth's crust (%)
Aluminium	8.1
Iron	6.3
Tin	0.00022
Copper	0.0068

a Which is the most abundant metal shown in the table?

_____ [1 mark]

b What percentage of the Earth's crust is tin?

Write your answer in standard form.

_____ [1 mark]

c Suggest a reason why it is more important to recycle tin than aluminium.

_____ [1 mark]

d Suggest **two** other factors that need to be considered when recycling.

_____

_____ [2 marks]

Answers

Section 1: Atomic structure and the periodic table

Atoms, elements and compounds

1. Oxygen [1 mark]
2. Ca [1 mark], Cl_2 [1 mark]
3. **a** iron [1 mark], carbon [1 mark]
   b iron oxide [1 mark], carbon dioxide [1 mark]
4. Contains two or more elements [1 mark] chemically combined [1 mark]

Mixtures

1. Numbering boxes 1 to 4 from top: 1 – 3 [1 mark], 2 – 1 [1 mark], 3 – 4 [1 mark], 4 – 2 [1 mark]
2. **a** Use a magnet. [1 mark] The iron will stick to the magnet, but the sulfur will not. [1 mark]
   b In the mixture the elements are not chemically combined together. [1 mark]

   In the compound the elements are chemically combined/can only be separated by a chemical reaction. [1 mark]

Compounds, formulae and equations

1. $NaNO_3$ [1 mark]
2. KI – potassium iodide [1 mark], MgS – magnesium sulfide [1 mark], $MgSO_4$ – magnesium sulfate [1 mark], Worked example answer given in workbook for the 4th mark.
3. carbon, chlorine, fluorine [3 marks]
4. magnesium chloride, Mg, H_2 [4 marks]

Scientific models of the atom

1. **a** plum pudding model [1 mark]
   b Answers in order: neutrally [1 mark], negatively [1 mark], electrons [1 mark]
2. Marks in three bands according to level of response.

Level 3 [5–6 marks]: A number of reasons have been given. Student considers both the meaning of the results and the validity of the experiment. They show a clear understanding of how new evidence leads to changes in models or theories.
Level 2 [3–4 marks]: A number of reasons have been given linked to why models change over time. Student mentions the validity of the experiment.
Level 1 [1–2 marks]: One or more reasons have been given.
Level 0 [0 marks]: No relevant content.

Points that should be made:

- New evidence was collected.
- The results showed the (plum pudding) model was not correct.
- The model had to change to explain the results.
- The data was checked by other scientists/it was reproducible.
- The conclusions drawn were valid.
- The experiment was well designed/carried out by scientists.

Sizes of atoms and molecules

1. $1000 – 1 \times 10^3$ [1 mark], $100 – 1 \times 10^2$ [1 mark], $11\,000 – 1.1 \times 10^4$ [1 mark], 1 million $– 1 \times 10^6$ [1 mark]
2. 2×10^{-10} m [1 mark]
3. Worked example – full answer given in workbook.
4. 150/10 000 [1 mark]

   0.015 m [1 mark]

   $0.015 \times 1000 = 15$ (mm) [1 mark]

Relative masses and charges of subatomic particles

1. **a** X – neutron [1 mark]; Y – proton [1 mark]; Z – electron [1 mark] –1 [1 mark]
   b They contain the same number of protons and electrons. [1 mark]
   c i 2 [1 mark]   **ii** 4 [1 mark]   **iii** He [1 mark]
2. Both contain 6 protons. [1 mark]

   Both contain 6 electrons. [1 mark]

   Carbon-12 contains 6 neutrons. [1 mark]

   Carbon-14 contains 8 neutrons. [1 mark]

Relative atomic mass

1. It has a mass number of 23. [1 mark]

   It has an atomic number of 11. [1 mark]
2. **a** 46 [1 mark]
   b Worked example – full answer given in workbook.
3. $35 \times 75 = 2625$ [1 mark] $37 \times 25 = 925$ [1 mark]

   $(2625 + 925) / 100$ [1 mark]

   Relative atomic mass of chlorine = 35.5 [1 mark]
4. An average of the atomic masses of all the isotopes of an element [1 mark] taking into account the relative abundances/percentage of each isotope. [1 mark]

Electronic structure

1. Numbering boxes 1 to 4 from top: 1 – 3 [1 mark], 2 – 2 [1 mark], 3– 4 [1 mark], 4 – 1 [1 mark]
2. Answers in order: nucleus, energy, two, eight. [4 marks]

98

3. **a** 2 electrons on innermost energy level [1 mark]

8 electrons on second energy level [1 mark]

b It has one more proton than electrons/it has 11 protons and 10 electrons [1 mark]

Protons have a positive charge and electrons have a negative charge [1 mark]

Electronic structure and the periodic table

1. In order of atomic number. [1 mark]

2. They have the same number of electrons on their outer shell. [1 mark]

3. **a** **i** W [1 mark] **ii** Z [1 mark]
iii Z [1 mark] **iv** X [1 mark]

b X and Y [1 mark]

Development of the periodic table

1. atomic weight [1 mark], groups [1 mark]

2. It is a metal. [1 mark]

It has a melting point of less than 660 °C (accept an estimation if more than 660 °C). [1 mark]

It has a density of more than 2.70 g/cm³ (accept an estimation if more than 2.70 g/cm³). [1 mark]

It will react with chlorine to form a compound that has the formula XCl_3. [1 mark]

Comparing metals and non-metals

1. Area to the right of the zig-zag is shaded. [1 mark]

2. **a** sodium + chlorine → sodium chloride [1 mark]

b Sodium – Metal [1 mark], Sodium chloride – Non-metal [1 mark], Chlorine – Non-metal [1 mark]

3. **a** B, C [2 marks] **b** B [1 mark]

c Electrical conductor, high melting/boiling point [2 marks]

Elements in group 0

1. They exist as single atoms. [1 mark] They have a full outer shell of electrons. [1 mark]

2. **a** $1.78 \times 10 = 17.8 = 18$ (g) (to 2 s.f.) [2 marks]

b All points plotted correctly [2 marks]. Award 1 mark if one point plotted incorrectly. Line of best fit drawn [1 mark]

3. They have a full outer shell of electrons. [1 mark] So do not have to lose or gain any electrons (to gain a full outer shell). [1 mark] So do not react/form molecules with other elements. [1 mark]

Elements in group 1

1. The alkali metals [1 mark]

2. **a** oxygen [1 mark]

b lithium hydroxide, hydrogen [2 marks]

c One from: safety glasses, tweezers, safety screen (or other sensible suggestion) [1 mark]

3. The sodium will go dull more quickly than lithium because it is more reactive. [1 mark]

4. Any **four** from:

Both form hydrogen.

Both form a hydroxide/alkali solution/the pH of the water will increase.

Both will move around the surface of the water.

Both will melt in the water.

The sodium forms sodium hydroxide, the lithium forms lithium hydroxide.

The sodium may give out a flame, the lithium will not.

The sodium will react more quickly than the lithium. [4 marks]

Elements in group 7

1. Bromine exists as pairs of atoms. [1 mark]

2. **a** fluorine/chlorine [1 mark]

b The boiling point increases. [1 mark]

3. When a group 7 element reacts with a metal it gains an electron. [1 mark] To form a stable arrangement/to fill its outer shell of electrons/to get 8 electrons on its outer shell. [1 mark] The electron is attracted to the positive nucleus. [1 mark] As you go down the group the atom gets larger. [1 mark] The outer shell is further from the nucleus/nucleus is shielded by more electron shells. [1 mark] The larger the atom, the weaker the force of attraction from the nucleus on the electron. [1 mark]

4. **a** bromine [1 mark], potassium chloride [1 mark]

b There is no displacement reaction occurring [1 mark] because iodine is less reactive than bromine [1 mark].

Section 2: Bonding, structure, and the properties of matter

The three states of matter

1. $CuO\ (s) + H_2SO_4\ (aq) \rightarrow CuSO_4\ (aq) + H_2O\ (l)$ [1 mark]

2. Boiling – C [1 mark], Condensing – D [1 mark], Freezing – A [1 mark], Melting – B [1 mark]

3. **a** Wait until the salol has turned into a liquid. [1 mark] Read the temperature using thermometer. [1 mark]

b Its melting point is too/very high. [1 mark] So they do not have the equipment to get it hot enough. [1 mark]

Ionic bonding and ionic compounds

1. sodium chloride (NaCl) [1 mark]

   lithium oxide (Li_2O) [1 mark]

2. a Ca^{2+} and O^{2-} [1mark]

   b i B [1 mark]

      ii Worked example – full answer given in workbook.

3. K_2S

   K and S [1 mark] in the correct ratio [1 mark]

Dot and cross diagrams for ionic compounds

1. a Ionic [1 mark]   b MgF_2 [1 mark]

2. Electrons transferred from sodium to oxygen. [1 mark] Two sodium atoms each lose one electron [1 mark] forming $Na^+/1+$ ions. [1 mark] Oxygen atoms gain 2 electrons [1 mark] forming $O^{2-}/2-$ ions. [1 mark]

Properties of ionic compounds

1. They have high boiling points. [1 mark]

   They are all solids at room temperature. [1 mark]

2. a   [1 mark]

   b Giant ionic lattice [1 mark]

3. Marks in three bands according to level of response.

Level 3 [5–6 marks]: Student explains all properties using sound knowledge of the bonding in an ionic compound.
Level 2 [3–4 marks]: Student explains some properties using correct knowledge of the bonding in an ionic compound.
Level 1 [1–2 marks]: Student explains one property correctly.
Level 0 [0 marks]: No relevant content.
Points that should be made: • There are strong forces between the ions.   • This comes about because of the attraction between positive and negative ions.   • The forces act in all directions.   • Large amounts of energy are needed to break the bonds and melt sodium chloride.   • When solid the ions cannot move.   • When melted the ions are free to move and so charge can flow.

Covalent bonding in small molecules

1. Carbon dioxide [1 mark], Water [1 mark]

2. Answers in order: share [1 mark], electrons [1 mark], strong [1 mark]

3. a Worked example – full answer given in workbook.

   b The boiling point increases. [1 mark]

4. One line from carbon to each hydrogen. [1 mark]

Dot and cross diagrams for covalent compunds

1. Numbering boxes 1 to 4 from top: 1 – 1 [1 mark], 2 – 4 [1 mark], 3 – 3 [1 mark], 4 – 2 [1 mark]

2. a Worked example – full answer given in workbook.

   b They do not show the 3D shape of the molecule. [1 mark]

3. Three shared pairs of electrons. [1 mark]

   One pair remaining on each atom. [1 mark]

Properties of small molecules

1. Normally gases or liquids at room temperature [1 mark] Do not conduct electricity when dissolved in water [1 mark]

2. carbon [1 mark], hydrogen [1 mark]

3. Covalent [1 mark]

4. The forces between the molecules (intermolecular forces) break. [1 mark]

Polymers

1. Plastic [1 mark]

2. One line drawn joining both chains. [1 mark]

3. The intermolecular forces are stronger in poly(ethene) (than ethene). [1 mark] So more heat energy is needed to break the forces [1 mark] and turn poly(ethene) into a gas. [1 mark]

4. a A [1 mark]

   b Polymer A cannot be stretched because the polymer chains cannot be moved apart [1 mark] because they are linked by strong cross-links. [1 mark]

Giant covalent structures

1. a Simple molecules: ammonia [1 mark], oxygen. [1 mark] Giant covalent structure: graphite [1 mark], silicon dioxide. [1 mark]

   b i diamond/graphite/oxygen. [1 mark]

      ii oxygen. [1 mark]

      iii diamond/graphite. [1 mark]

2. Graphite [1 mark], diamond [1 mark], silicon dioxide/silica [1 mark]

3. Any **four** from:

Silicon dioxide has a giant covalent structure.

Carbon dioxide is made up of simple molecules.

There are strong covalent bonds between the silicon and oxygen atoms in silicon dioxide.

All bonds in silicon dioxide are strong covalent bonds.

There are strong covalent bonds between the carbon and oxygen atoms in the carbon dioxide.

There are weak intermolecular forces between the carbon dioxide molecules. [4 marks]

Properties of giant covalent structures

1. High melting and boiling point [1 mark]

2. Strong covalent bonds [1 mark] between all (carbon) atoms. [1 mark]

3. **a** Any **one** from: Both contain carbon atoms. Both have strong covalent bonds between atoms. [1 mark]

   b Metal [1 mark]

   c There are (delocalised) electrons between the layers [1 mark] which can move/carry charge [1 mark]

Graphene and fullerenes

1. **a** Graphene [1 mark], Carbon nanotube [1 mark]

   b 6 [1 mark]

   c Any **one** from: electrical circuits, catalysts, reinforcing materials [1 mark]

   d Property e.g. high electrical conductivity, large surface area, high strength. [1 mark]

   Explanation: e.g. allows electricity to pass through, more chance the reactants will collide, increase the force needed to break the material [1 mark]

2. **a** 1×10^{-8} m [1 mark]

   b 10 nm $\times$ 100 000 [1 mark]

   1 000 000 nm [1 mark]

   1 000 000 $\times$ 0.000001 = 1 mm [1 mark]

Metallic bonding

1. Cobalt [1 mark], Copper [1 mark]

2. It is strong [1 mark]

3. positive ion [1 mark], sea of electrons [1 mark]

4. They are not attached to any particular atom. [1 mark] They are free to move. [1 mark]

5. There is a strong force of attraction [1 mark] between positive metal ions [1 mark] and the 'sea' of negative electrons. [1 mark]

Properties of metals and alloys

1. bronze [1 mark]

2. A mixture [1 mark] of different metals. [1 mark]

3. It has atoms of different sizes added [1 mark] which prevents the layers sliding over each other. [1 mark]

4. **a** The melting points of group 2 metals are higher than the melting points of group 1 metals. [1 mark]

   b Group 2 metals have two electrons on their outer shell/the delocalised electrons in group 2 metals contain two electrons from each atom. [1 mark] Group 1 metals have one electron on their outer shell/the delocalised electrons in group 1 metals contain one electron from each atom. [1 mark] There are more delocalised electrons in group 2 metals. [1 mark] So the metallic bonds are stronger in group 2 metals than group 1 metals, so more heat energy is needed to break them. [1 mark]

Section 3: Quantitative chemistry

Writing formulae

1. BF_3 [1 mark]

2. PbO_2 [1 mark]

3. **a** 3 [1 mark]   **b** 4 [1 mark]   **c** 11 [1 mark]

4. **a** Any one from: Use a gas syringe. Use a delivery tube into an upturned measuring cylinder/burette full of water. [1 mark]

   Accept a labelled diagram

   b Calcium carbonate – $CaCO_3$ [1 mark], Calcium chloride – $CaCl_2$ [1 mark], Carbon dioxide – CO_2 [1 mark]

Conservation of mass and balanced chemical equations

1. lost [1 mark], chemical reaction [1 mark], equal to [1 mark]

2. 2.3 + 1.2 [1 mark] = 3.5 g [1 mark]

3. The product is not water. [1 mark]

   $2H_2 + O_2$ [1 mark] $\rightarrow 2H_2O$ [1 mark]

Mass changes when a reactant or product is a gas

1. 4.2 – 3 = 1.2 g [1 mark]

2. **a** Thermal decomposition [1 mark]

   b Worked example – full answer given in workbook.

   c **i** Worked example – full answer given in workbook.

      ii (0.8 + 0.5 + 0.9 + 0.4 + 0.6)/5 = 0.64 [1 mark]
      (0.5/0.64) $\times$ 100 [1 mark] = 78.1% [1 mark]

Relative formula mass

1. 32 [1 mark]

2. From top, lines to: 81 [1 mark], 44 [1 mark], 98 [1 mark], 18 [1 mark]

3. M_r of 2KI = 2 $\times$ (39 + 127) = 332 [1 mark]

   M_r of $Pb(NO_3)_2$ = 207 + (14 $\times$ 2) + (16 $\times$ 6) = 331 [1 mark]

Total M_r of reactants = 332 + 331 = 663 [1 mark]

M_r of PbI_2 = 207 + (2 × 127) = 461 [1 mark]

M_r of $2KNO_3$ = 2 x (39 + 14 + (16 × 3)) = 202 [1 mark]

Total M_r of products = 461 + 202 = 663 [1 mark]

Moles

1. 46 g [1 mark]

2. 1.5 [1 mark]

3. **a** 4 × 12 = 48 g [1 mark]

   b Worked example – full answer given in workbook.

   c 1 + 80 = 81 [1 mark]

   283.5/81 = 3.5 moles [1 mark]

4. $6.02 × 10^{23}$ [1 mark]

Amounts of substances in equations

1. **a** M_r calcium carbonate = 40 + 12 + (16 × 3) = 100 [1 mark]

   200/100 = 2 (moles) [1 mark]

   b M_r calcium oxide = 40 + 16 = 56 [1 mark]

   56 × 2 (moles) = 112 (kg) [1 mark]

2. **a** To prevent the mixture coming out of the test tube [1 mark] and causing burns. [1 mark]

   b M_r copper oxide = 2 × (63.5 + 16) = 159 [1 mark]

   Moles copper oxide = 1.59/159 = 0.01 [1 mark]

   Mass copper = (63.5 x 2) × 0.01 [1 mark]

   = 1.27 (g)

Using moles to balance equations

1. 0.1 [1 mark]

2. **a** iron + chlorine → iron chloride [1 mark]

   b 1.12/56 = 0.02 [1 mark]

   2.13/(35.5 × 2) = 0.03 [1 mark]

   c $2Fe + 3Cl_2$ [1 mark] → $2FeCl_3$ [1 mark]

Limiting reactants

1. Answers in order: chemical, limiting, excess [3 marks]

2. Potassium [1 mark]

3. **a** A colour change/some of the copper oxide was used up. [1 mark]

   b Copper oxide [1 mark] because there was some left over after the reaction had finished. [1 mark]

Concentration of solutions

1. 1000 [1 mark]

2. 1 g of salt in 2 cm^3 of water [1 mark]

3. **a** 15/100 = 0.15 (g/cm^3) [1 mark]

   b 10 cm^3/1000 = 0.01 dm^3 [1 mark]

   0.2/0.01 = 20 (g/dm^3) [1 mark]

   c 50 cm^3/1000 = 0.05 dm^3 [1 mark]

   0.05 × 10 = 0.5 g [1 mark]

Section 4: Chemical changes

Metal oxides

1. magnesium + oxygen → magnesium oxide [1 mark]

   zinc + oxygen → zinc(II) oxide [1 mark]

2. Answers in order: oxides, oxidation [2 marks]

3. **a** copper oxide [1 mark]

   b $2Cu + O_2 → 2CuO$ [2 marks]

   c The inside did not come into contact with oxygen [1 mark], so no copper oxide/CuO was formed. [1 mark]

Reactivity series

1. potassium hydroxide [1 mark], hydrogen [1 mark]

2. magnesium [1 mark], hydrogen [1 mark]

3. **a** A, C, D, B [2 marks]

   b B [1 mark] because it does not react with acid or water [1 mark]

   c Worked example – full answer given in workbook.

Reactivity series – displacement

1. Magnesium [1 mark]

2. **a** Worked example – full answer given in workbook.

   b iron [1 mark], copper [1 mark]

3. chromium, cobalt, nickel [1 mark]

   Cobalt can displace nickel from its solution (so must be more reactive than nickel). [1 mark]

   Chromium can displace cobalt from its solution (so must be more reactive than cobalt). [1 mark]

Extraction of metals

1. In a compound, with other elements [1 mark]

2. iron – reduction with carbon [1 mark], aluminium – electrolysis [1 mark], sodium – electrolysis [1 mark], lead – reduction with carbon [1 mark]

3. **a** zinc oxide [1 mark]

   b carbon [1 mark]

   c For 2 marks, any **one** from:

   Quarrying of zinc oxide [1 mark] can destroy habitats/reduce biodiversity. [1 mark]

Carbon dioxide is produced which is a greenhouse gas [1 mark] and contributes to climate change. [1 mark]

Carbon/zinc oxide are limited resources [1 mark] so supplies will run out in the future. [1 mark]

Oxidation and reduction in terms of electrons

1. A metal loses electrons to form ions. [1 mark]
2. $Na^+ + e^- \rightarrow Na$ – Reduction [1 mark], $2Cl^- \rightarrow 2e^- + Cl_2$ – Oxidation [1 mark], $Zn - 2e^- \rightarrow Zn^{2+}$ – Oxidation [1 mark], $2F^- - 2e^- \rightarrow F_2$ – Oxidation [1 mark]
3. 4 [1 mark]
4. a $2CuO$ [1 mark] $+ C$ [1 mark] $\rightarrow 2Cu + CO_2$ [1 mark]
   b $2Cu^{2+} + 2e^- \rightarrow Cu$ [1 mark]

Reactions of acids with metals

1. Metal: Zinc [1 mark], Acid: Sulfuric acid [1 mark]
2. a magnesium chloride [1 mark]
   b Worked example – full answer given in workbook.
   c Collect the gas. [1 mark] Add a lighted splint. [1 mark] There will be a squeaky pop noise. [1 mark]
   d $Mg + 2HCl \rightarrow MgCl_2 + H_2$ (one mark for each correct reactant/product) for 4 marks in total

Neutralisation of acids and making salts

1. They are insoluble. [1 mark]
   They neutralise acids. [1 mark]
2. potassium chloride [1 mark]
3. calcium oxide + sulfuric acid – calcium sulfate + water [1 mark], calcium carbonate + sulfuric acid – calcium sulfate + water + carbon dioxide [1 mark], calcium oxide + nitric acid – calcium nitrate + water [1 mark], Worked example answer given in workbook for the 4th mark.
4. Nitric acid [1 mark]
   Potassium hydroxide [1 mark]

Making soluble salts

1. a Hazard:
   Any **one** from: Acid in eyes
   Burns from Bunsen burner/glassware [1 mark]
   Way of reducing the risk of harm:
   Answer should be a sensible way of reducing the risk from the hazard mentioned: e.g. Wear eye protection/ let equipment cool before touching it. [1 mark]
   b There will be unreacted copper oxide in the beaker. [1 mark]
   c Copper sulfate [1 mark]

d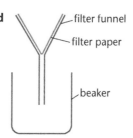

Filter funnel [1 mark], Filter paper [1 mark]
e Filtration/filtering [1 mark]

2. a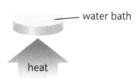

   [2 marks]
   b The water will evaporate from the solution. [1 mark]
   The salt will remain in the dish. [1 mark]
   Award 1 mark for 'the water will be removed'.

pH and neutralisation

1. H^+ [1 mark]
2. Universal indicator [1 mark], pH probe [1 mark]
3. 1–6 – Acidic [1 mark], 7 – Neutral [1 mark], 8–14 – Alkaline [1 mark]
4. $H^+ (aq) + OH^- (aq) \rightarrow H_2O (l)$ [2 marks]
5. a Add universal indicator to the sodium hydroxide. [1 mark] Add small amounts of acid, mixing [1 mark] until the indicator just turns green. [1 mark]
   b Any one from: It is difficult to tell when the solution is just neutral/no precise colour change. It dyes the salt solution/needs to be removed. [1 mark]

Strong and weak acids

1. fully ionises [1 mark], H^+ ions [1 mark], nitric [1 mark]
2. Numbering boxes on the left from the top:
   1 – Strong and dilute [1 mark], 2 – Weak and dilute [1 mark], 3 – Weak and concentrated [1 mark], 4 – Strong and concentrated [1 mark]
3. It decreases/goes down [1 mark] because the number of hydrogen ions increases. [1 mark]

The process of electrolysis

1. a C [1 mark]   b B [1 mark]
   c So the ions are free to move [1 mark]

2. Arrow drawn from negative ion to the positive electrode. [1 mark] Arrow drawn from positive ion to the negative electrode. [1 mark]

3. Answers in order: electrodes, cathode, anode, elements [4 marks]

Electrolysis of molten ionic compounds

1. Sodium chloride (NaCl) [1 mark], Calcium oxide (CaO) [1 mark]

2. Anode: fluorine [1 mark], Cathode: potassium [1 mark]

3. **a** The ions (in the lead(II) bromide) are free to move [1 mark] to conduct electricity [1 mark] and complete the circuit. [1 mark]

   b Bromide ions are attracted to the positive electrode. [1 mark] Bromine gas is being formed. [1 mark]

Using electrolysis to extract metals

1. They are more reactive than carbon. [1 mark]

2. **a** Aluminium ions have a positive charge. [1 mark] They are attracted to the (negative) cathode. [1 mark]

   b Negative oxygen ions/O^{2-} ions [1 mark] are attracted to the anodes [1 mark] and react to form carbon dioxide. [1 mark]

3. Marks in three bands according to level of response.

Level 3 [5–6 marks]: Student compares associated energy costs of recycling and extracting aluminium with examples of where energy is used.
Level 2 [3–4 marks]: Student compares some associated energy costs of recycling and extracting aluminium.
Level 1 [1–2 marks]: Student states some energy costs of recycling and extracting aluminium.
Level 0 [0 marks]: No relevant points made.

Points that should be included:

Recycling:

- Uses less energy than extracting aluminium.
- Energy is used to transport the collected aluminium from homes/businesses to the recycling plant.
- Energy is used to sort the aluminium from other metals.
- Energy is used to melt the metal.

Extracting aluminium:

- Energy is used to mine the aluminium oxide, transport and process it.
- Energy is used to melt the aluminium oxide.
- Cryolite is added to the aluminium oxide to reduce the melting point and reduce energy costs.
- A lot of electricity is used to carry out electrolysis.
- Generating electricity also has energy costs.

Electrolysis of aqueous solutions

1. **a** Sulfate and hydroxide [1 mark]

   b Prediction: The electrode will be covered in copper/copper will be formed. [1 mark]

   Reason: Copper is less reactive than hydrogen [1 mark]

2. Diagram [4 marks]:

   Two inert/graphite electrodes

   In beaker of sodium chloride solution

   In electrical circuit containing power supply

   One electrode connected to the negative terminal and one connected to the positive

   Add lighted splint to gas produced at the cathode. [1 mark]

   If hydrogen is present then there will be a squeaky pop noise. [1 mark]

Half equations at electrodes

1. 1: Sodium [1 mark], 2: Chlorine (do not accept 'chloride') [1 mark]

2. **a** A [1 mark]   **b** B [1 mark]   **c** B [1 mark]

3. Answers in order: cathode [1 mark], electrons [1 mark], reduction [1 mark]

4. **a** $2e^-$ [1 mark]   **b** $4OH^-$ [1 mark]

Section 5: Energy changes in reactions

Exothermic and endothermic reactions

1. Answers in order: conserved [1 mark], exothermic [1 mark], energy [1 mark], increases [1 mark], more [1 mark]

2. Sports injury packs [1 mark]

3. **a** and **b**: Worked example – full answers given in workbook.

4. **a**   [4 marks]

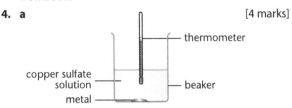

thermometer

copper sulfate solution

beaker

metal

   b Any **two** from: concentration of copper sulfate, volume of copper sulfate, mass of metal, size of metal particles [2 marks]

   c Any **two** from: measuring cylinder, balance, also accept lid [2 marks]

   d i Result: 4.3 [1 mark]

   Reason: any **one** from: misread the thermometer; didn't wait long enough before taking the reading; used very cold copper sulfate [1 mark]

   ii 4.0 [1 mark]

iii In order of increasing reactivity: zinc, magnesium, calcium [2 marks]

iv Use a lid to stop heat energy escaping from the top of the beaker. [1 mark]

Wrap cotton wool around the beaker to insulate it and reduce heat loss. [1 mark]

Use a polystyrene cup to improve insulation and reduce heat loss. [1 mark]

Use a temperature sensor to record the temperature. This should lead to a more accurate result as many more data points will be collected. [1 mark]

Allow any other reasonable answer.

Reaction profiles

1. The reacting particles must collide. [1 mark]

The reacting particles must have enough energy to activate the reaction. [1 mark]

2. a reactants [1 mark], products [1 mark], activation energy [1 mark], energy change during the reaction [1 mark]

b The energy of the products is lower than that of the reactants. [1 mark]

c The line drawn showing the energy level of the products would be higher than that of the reactants. [1 mark] The arrow showing the overall energy change would go up. [1 mark]

3. The activation energy is the energy needed to start the reaction between propane gas and oxygen. [1 mark] They could turn on the gas, strike a match [1 mark] and hold it in the gas. The energy given out from the burning match is transferred to the reacting particles of propane and oxygen. [1 mark]

Energy change of reactions

1. a Bonds break C–H and O$=$O. (1 mark)

Atoms rearrange. [1 mark]

Bonds made C$=$O and H–O [1 mark]

Accept if answer is given in terms of correct coloured particles e.g. bonds break between yellow and purple particle, etc.

b Worked example – full answer given in workbook.

c Bond energies of reactants = $(8 \times$ C–H$)$ + $(2 \times$ C–C$)$ + $(5 \times$ O$=$O$)$ = 3296 + 692 + 2490 = 6478 kJ/mol. [2 marks]

Bond energies of products = $3(2 \times$ C$=$O$)$ + $4(2 \times$ O–H$)$ = 3192 + 3720 = 6912 kJ/mol. [2 marks]

Energy given out during the reaction is 6912 – 6478 = 434 kJ/mol. [1 mark]

Therefore, propane gives out more energy than methane when it burns in oxygen. [1 mark]

Section 6: Rates of reactions

Measuring rates of reaction

1. Numbering boxes on left-hand side from the top: 1 – The loss of mass over time [1 mark], 2 – The volume of gas produced over time [1 mark], 3 – The time for a solution to become cloudy, 4 – The volume of gas produced over time [1 mark]

Calculating rates of reaction

1. a Mean rate of reaction = (quantity of product formed / time taken). [1 mark]

b Unit of quantity: cm^3 [1 mark], Unit of rate: g/s [1 mark]

c Mean rate of reaction = 15/20 = 0.75 cm^3/s [2 marks]

d 1 mark for correctly labelling axis; 3 marks for correctly plotting all the points; 1 mark for drawing a smooth line; 3 marks for correctly marking areas of graph. [8 marks]

2. a Worked example – full answer given in workbook.

b Slope of gradient = 35/25 = 1.28 cm^3/s [1 mark]

Effect of concentration and pressure

1. a i B [1 mark], There are fewer reacting red particles in B than in A. [1 mark]

ii A [1 mark], Increasing the concentration of a reactant increases the chances of a successful collision. [1 mark]

b increase the pressure [1 mark]

2. a i A stop-clock [1 mark]

ii Mix the sodium thiosulfate and hydrochloric acid in a beaker. [1 mark] Put the beaker on a black cross. [1 mark]

Time how long it will take for the cross to disappear. [1 mark]

b i By adding more concentrated acid to the dilute acid. [1 mark]

He will need to use a measuring cylinder to make sure he keeps the volume the same. [1 mark]

ii It will decrease. [1 mark]

Effect of surface area

1. Answers in order: collision [1 mark], activation [1 mark], frequency [1 mark], increase [1 mark]

2. a To control the variable [1 mark]

b A – powder calcium carbonate, B – small chips of calcium carbonate, C – single chip of calcium carbonate [3 marks]

c i 2.20 g [1 mark]   **ii** 1.10 g [1 mark]

d Increase the surface area of a reactant, increase the rate of reaction. [1 mark]

e The reaction stopped here because it had used up one of the reactants. [2 marks]

Effect of temperature

1. Increasing the temperature decreases the rate of reaction. [1 mark]

Increasing the temperature increases the potential energy of the reacting particles. [1 mark]

2. a 40 s too low [1 mark]

b Repeat the experiment [1 mark]

c T2 is higher than T1 [1 mark] because it took a shorter time for the reaction to stop. [1 mark]

d Mean rate of reaction = volume of gas collected / time = 63/50 = 1.26 cm³/s [3 marks]

e It is fastest at the start [1 mark] and then gradually slows down. [1 mark]

Effect of catalyst

1. Answers in order: catalysts [1 mark], speed [1 mark], used [1 mark], specific [1 mark]

2. a water oxygen [1 mark]

b Marks in three bands according to level of response.

Level 3 [5–6 marks]: There is a clear, balanced and detailed description of an experimental procedure and explanation of how a catalyst works.
Level 2 [3–4 marks]: There is some description of an experimental procedure and explanation of how a catalyst works.
Level 1 [1–2 marks]: There is a brief description of an experimental procedure and explanation of how a catalyst works.
Level 0 [0 marks]: No relevant content.

Points that should be made:

- A catalyst speeds up a reaction without taking part.
- Catalysts lower the activation energy of a reaction.
- Catalysts increase the chances of a successful collision between reactant particles (due to lower activation energy).
- The overall reaction profile stays the same as the energy of the reactant particles and product particles does actually change.

- Measure the time it takes to collect 40 cm³ (or fixed amount) of oxygen gas.
- Collect the gas in a gas syringe.
- Collect the gas by displacement with water using an upturned measuring cylinder full of water.
- Carry out the reaction in a conical flask connected to a delivery tube and a way of collecting the gas.
- Repeat using different catalysts until the best one is found.
- Carefully record the results.

c i To act as a control – so they have a control to compare the other results to. [1 mark]

ii Manganese oxide [1 mark] because it produced the gas quickest. [1 mark]

iii

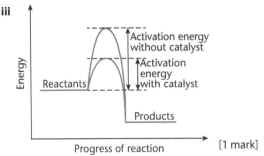

[1 mark]

Reversible reactions and energy changes

1. a ammonia + hydrogen chloride → ammonium chloride [1 mark]

b ammonium chloride → ammonia + hydrogen chloride [1 mark]

c The reaction is reversible. [1 mark]

d Heat it to get the forward reaction [1 mark]; cool it to get the reverse reaction. [1 mark]

e $NH_4Cl\,(s) \rightleftharpoons NH_3\,(g) + HCl\,(g)$ [3 marks]

2. a The white powder will go blue again. [1 mark]

b It is exothermic. [1 mark]

c Endothermic. [1 mark] The energy change for both directions is the same. [1 mark]

Equilibrium and Le Chatelier's Principle

1. Answers in order: reversible [1 mark], closed [1 mark], equilibrium [1 mark], rate [1 mark]

2. In a closed bottle, no gas can escape so the system is closed and equilibrium can be reached. [2 marks] The glass is open so carbon dioxide gas can escape as soon as it forms. This means that more gas will be made as the reverse reaction is favoured. [2 marks]

3. Effects of changing the temperature on a system. [1 mark] Effects of changing the pressure on a system [1 mark]

4. The system will respond by making more A and B, to reduce the concentration of C. [2 marks]

Changing the position of equilibrium

1. **a** 1, 3, 2 [2 marks]

   b Increasing the pressure – equilibrium moves to the right [1 mark], Changing the catalyst – no change of position of equilibrium [1 mark], Increasing the temperature – equilibrium moves to the left [1 mark]

2. **a** 2 [1 mark], 2 [1 mark]

   b SO_3 [1 mark]

   c It would move to the left [1 mark] as two molecules would rearrange into three molecules. [1 mark]

   d Lowering the temperature, increases the % conversion to SO_3 from SO_2 [1 mark]

   The reaction is exothermic [1 mark], so lower temperatures shift the equilibrium towards the forward reaction. [1 mark]

Section 7: Organic chemistry

Crude oil and hydrocarbons

1. Answers in order: finite [1 mark], plankton [1 mark], biomass [1 mark]

2. coal [1 mark], natural gas [1 mark]

Structure and formulae of alkanes

1. Answers in order: homologous [1 mark], single [1 mark], four [1 mark], one [1 mark]

2. CH_4 [1 mark]

3. second row: Ethane, H—C—C—H [1 mark], third row: 3,

   fourth row: Butane, C_4H_{10} [1 mark]

4. **i** C_5H_{12} [1 mark]   **ii** C_8H_{18} [1 mark]

Fractional distillation and petrochemicals

1. true [1 mark], false [1 mark]

2. C_2H_6, C_3H_8, C_4H_{10} [1 mark]

3. **a, b, c**   [2 marks]

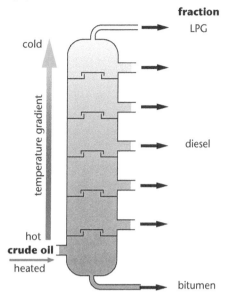

d Fuel oil is a much bigger molecule than petrol and so has a higher boiling point than petrol [1 mark]. All fractions boil and the vapours rise up the column [1 mark]. Those with higher boiling points condense first and so are collected near the bottom of the column [1 mark].

Combustion of fuels

1. **a** oxygen [1 mark]

   b carbon dioxide [1 mark]

   c water [1 mark]

   d Black is carbon or soot due to some incomplete combustion. [2 marks]

   e carbon dioxide, water [1 mark]

   f 2, 2 [1 mark]

Cracking and alkenes

1. **a** the porous pot [1 mark]

   b To get it to work, it must be hot enough to break the strong bond. [1 mark]

   c i The bromine water changes from orange to colourless. [1 mark]

   ii The first test tube may have been full of air that was in the apparatus at the start of the experiment. [1 mark]

   Alkenes had been made as shown by test 2 and 3 and, once all the air had been removed, it was collected. [1 mark]

   iii The bromine water remained orange. [1 mark]

2. The demand for petrol is much greater than that for kerosene. [1 mark] The supply of kerosene from crude oil is much greater than petrol. [1 mark] When kerosene is cracked, petrol is formed thus meeting the supply. [1 mark] By building the cracking plant near to the oil refinery transport costs are reduced. [1 mark]

Pure substances, mixtures and formulations

1. potassium bromide solution [1 mark]
2. **a** B [1 mark]   **b**   A and B [2 marks]
   c C [1 mark]
3. Ticks in: first row – Fractional distillation
   [1 mark], second row – Crystallisation [1 mark], third row
   – Filtration [1 mark]

Chromatography and R_f values

1. **a** Ink is a mixture and so the line would separate as well.
   [1 mark]
   b If it was higher the ink would smudge/start to separate
   too soon. [1 mark]
   c i 3 [1 mark]
   ii As the solvent moved up through the paper, it carried
   the dissolved dyes with it. [1 mark] Each
   dye travelled a different distance [1 mark] due
   to the different forces of attraction between the
   different dyes and chromatography paper or
   solvent. [1 mark]
2. **a**, **b**, **c**, **d** and **e**: Worked example – full answers given in
   workbook.

Tests for common gases

1. **a** Take conical flask off the balance and put a delivery
   tube in the top. [1 mark] Fill the water trough half
   full with water and place the delivery tube in the
   water. [1 mark] Fill the boiling tube with water and
   place it over the end of the delivery tube and collect
   the gas. [1 mark] When boiling tube is full put a
   bung in the end to stop the gas from escaping.
   [1 mark]
   b The gas is not oxygen. [1 mark]
   c The gas is carbon dioxide. [1 mark]
   d Re-do the limewater test; check with someone else.
   [1 mark]

The Earth's atmosphere – now and in the past

1. Ammonia [1 mark]
2. **a** Any **one** of: The evidence is limited.
   Scientists must rely on models built on
   assumptions.

Students only need to write down one point to
get the mark. [1 mark]
b CO_2 = 95%   95/100   19/20
Nitrogen and other gases = 5% 5/100 1/20
Ratio = 19:1 [2 marks]
c Because it is nearly all carbon dioxide, which is similar
to some of the current theories about Earth. [1 mark]

Changes in oxygen and carbon dioxide

1. **a** photosynthesis [1 mark]
   b carbon dioxide [1 mark], glucose [1 mark]
   c Carbon dioxide levels decreased as plants used it up.
   [1 mark] Oxygen levels increased as plants made it.
   [1 mark]
   d When all the iron was used up the reaction stopped
   [1 mark] and so as more oxygen was made it went into
   the atmosphere. [1 mark]
2. 1, 4, 3, 5, 2 [2 marks]

Greenhouse gases

1. oxygen [1 mark]
2. **a** [2 marks]

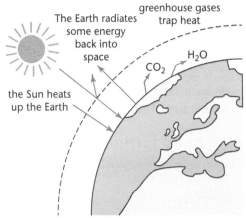

b Solar radiation has a short wavelength. [1 mark]
Radiation radiated back from Earth has a longer
wavelength. [1 mark]
c It is needed to keep the planet warm. [1 mark]
3. **a** parts per million [1 mark]
   b i it was 370ppm in 2000 and 390ppm in 2010. [1 mark]
          So increase is 390 – 370 = 20 ppm [1 mark]
      ii 410 ppm [1 mark]
   c Increase in the combustion of fossil fuels. [1 mark]
   Increase in deforestation. [1 mark]

Global climate change

1. More frequent and severe storms [1 mark]
2. **a** Temperature stress for humans and wildlife – It will
   be too hot to make a living [1 mark], Water stress for
   humans and wildlife – No fresh water supplies in some

areas [1 mark], Changes to food production capacity – Changes in agriculture i.e. what crops will grow [1 mark], Changes to distribution of wildlife – Migration patterns change [1 mark]

  b They may have to migrate to a different country if no water supply. [1 mark] Look to farm different crops that will grow in the new climate. [1 mark] Adapt building so they will cope with hotter temperatures and more extreme weather. [1 mark] Accept any other reasonable answer.

Carbon footprint and its reduction

1. Answers in order: footprint [1 mark], dioxide [1 mark], greenhouse [1 mark]
2. a Double glazed window [1 mark], Cavity wall insulation [1 mark]
   b Worked example – full answer given in workbook.

Air pollution from burning fuels

1. a Carbon dioxide – burning fossil fuels in power stations or combustion engines [1 mark]
   b Carbon particulates – incomplete combustion of coal or other fossil fuels [1 mark]
   c Sulfur dioxide – burning coal in power stations and combustion engines [1 mark]
   d Nitrogen monoxide – results from high temperatures in combustion engines [1 mark]
2. a and b: Worked example – full answers given in workbook.

Section 10: Using resources

What does the Earth provide for us?

1. Answer in order: renewable [1 mark], finite [1 mark], environment [1 mark]
2. Managed forest [1 mark]
3. second column: paper [1 mark], third column, from the top: PVC [1 mark], polystyrene [1 mark], nylon [1 mark]
4. Any points given below or other appropriate answers [4 marks in total, 1 mark for each]

   Wood from a managed source is a natural, renewable, sustainable source but will eventually rot if not painted or treated.

   Plastic is made from crude oil, a non-renewable source, which will eventually run out. The plastic is very durable, does not have to be maintained but will eventually go to landfill. Making the plastic involves industrial processes which will use up a lot of energy.

   I would choose the wood as overall I think it is better for the environment.

Safe drinking water

1. a [1 mark]

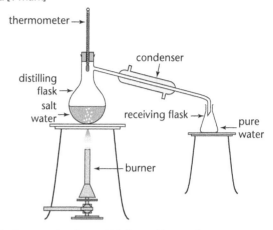

  b Evaporation [1 mark] followed by condensation. [1 mark]
  c Measure the boiling point to see if it is 100 °C. [1 mark] Test the pH to see if it is 7. [1 mark]
  d Any **one** of: Needs lots of energy. Requires specialist equipment. [1 mark]

Waste water treatment

1. a Water from the oceans evaporates; it condenses to form clouds, clouds move over high ground where it precipitates or rains back to the ground to fill rivers, lakes, reservoirs etc. [3 marks]
   b To stop people/animals from getting ill and prevent plants from dying. [1 mark]
2. a Answers in order: sewage [1 mark], organic [1 mark], microbes [1 mark], chemicals [1 mark]
   b Eutrophication in rivers and lakes. [1 mark]
   c Toxic chemicals could get into the natural water cycle/ enter into drinking water supply. [1 mark]

Life cycle assessment (LCA)

1. a Answers in order: assess [1 mark], products [1 mark], reduction [1 mark]
   b i Reusable nappies [1 mark] because the impact per baby per year is less. [1 mark] Reusable nappies use less energy during production; waste less water, use less raw materials and produce less domestic waste than disposable nappies. [1 mark]
     ii Disposable nappies will go to landfill. [1 mark] Reusable nappies may be recycled or they too could go to landfill. [1 mark]
   c It could be biased if a company wants to sell a lot of products. [1 mark]

Ways of reducing the use of resources

1. Reduce – Use less to avoid waste [1 mark], Reuse – Use the object again instead of throwing it away [1 mark], Recycle – Methods for making new materials from ones that have already been used [1 mark],

2. **a** aluminium [1 mark]

   b 2.2×10^{-4} [1 mark]

   c There is a lot more aluminium in the Earth's crust than tin. [1 mark]

   d Any **two** from: Energy used for recycling versus energy used for extraction. Cost of recycling versus cost of extraction. Ease of separating materials that need to be recycled. Any other suitable answer. [2 marks]